Raising Starfish

Connective Strategies for Childhood Dissociation

Rachel Heinbaugh

Raising Starfish: Connective Strategies for Childhood Dissociation

Rachel Heinbaugh

Cover Illustration: ProdesignsX

ISBN: 979-8-9882930-0-2

This book is not a replacement for therapy or professional help. This book expresses the viewpoint and gained knowledge of the author- this is not treatment. Any information about medications and therapies should be consulted with the appropriate professionals. The author shall not be held liable or responsible for loss or damage allegedly arising from any information or suggestion in this book.

Raising Starfish

Welcome! You may be a parent of a child with unexplainable behaviors, a biological parent, an adoptive parent, a foster parent, a teacher, a caregiver, or a clinician. You may have a house full of people with varying diagnoses, or you "feel" like something is off. You may be an adult who experienced extensive childhood traumas and want to be a "better" parent. You may be an adult who experienced ongoing pains and continue to struggle with traditional therapy forms. A well-meaning friend may have given you this book and you don't know what it has to do with you. I am glad you are here.

Neil Gaiman's "Anansi Boys" provides a fitting metaphor for childhood dissociation. The series follows the journey of Charlie and Spider, brothers whose paths are chaotically linked. They are like the antithesis of each other, good vs. evil, boring vs. fun, and light vs. shadow. In childhood, they were one child but a witch, Mrs. Dunwiddy, thought she could cast the shadow or trickster out of the boy. Now as adults, they discover that they are not fated to follow in the footsteps of their father, Anansi, nor are they destined to be entangled in connection with each other.

"Charlie said, 'You're not the magical bit of me, you know.' 'I'm not?' Spider took another step. Stars were falling now by the dozen, streaking their way across the dark sky. Someone, somewhere was playing high sweet music on a flute. Another step, and now distant sirens were blaring. 'No,' said Charlie. 'You're not. Mrs. Dunwiddy thought you were, I think. She split us apart, but she never really understood what she was doing. We're more like two halves of a starfish. You grew up into a whole person. And so,' he said, realizing it was true as he said it, 'did I.'"

Much like Charlie and Spider, children and adults in our world have lived in environments that cause them to split and regrow. Their internal life may have a variety of fully developed personalities, or their internal life may be slightly disconnected. Just as the environment (temperature, location, etc.) impacts how the starfish reforms or does not reconnect, our environment affects the inner development of humans. This book explores the role of dissociation in childhood behaviors and family interactions. It contains practical strategies, self- reflection prompts, and personal stories to help empower your journey. Whether you were that starfish child or are a caregiver of a starfish child - may this book provide a new lens to create a curious and compassion- ate environment through which we can cultivate an intentional connection with our inner self and others.

Because this book discusses trauma, go at a pace that fits you. I phrase scenarios in a vague format- walking a fine line between giving too much information and not enough for those needing help understanding. If you feel yourself experiencing stress, take a break- be compassionate. Feel free to jump sections or revisit a chapter later if a paragraph seems too much. This book contains triggering information.

I use neutral pronouns to protect the privacy of individuals. Some stories are specific to my family or people I know, and some are a general composite based on people I know. If you are confused by "they/them,"- take a deep breath and focus on the story's purpose. I find it helpful to remind myself of the goal: "I will gladly use neutral pronouns if it protects other people."

The content is from my personal experiences and learnings. This book does not replace a counselor; I am not a therapist. There are resources and suggestions that inform what mode of treatment you pursue. This book is not diagnostic but intended to give insight into what is often overlooked by caregivers and professionals. I strongly encourage exploring, researching, and finding what works for you and your family.

Lastly, my spouse and I absorbed, practiced, and integrated these approaches over several years. If the information seems too much, know that small steps generate a different trajectory over time. This approach is not a quick fix- it is a long-term transformation. You can be desperate and brave. Awful and kind. Damned and blessed. Two things can be true at the same time. I invite you on this challenging and good journey- You and your family are worth it.

CONTENTS

1

Introduction

Several years into our adoption journey, my family's progress was two steps forward and four steps back. With every positive behavioral growth, there were significant behaviors that increased anxiety. As parents, we were learning new strategies but barely treading water. The laundry of seven humans is enough to overwhelm, let alone the rest of parenting. Our five children were alive, fed, taken care of, playing, and getting good grades- yet emotionally were on thin ice. We addressed our parenting style, medication merry-go-round, self-care, and behavior charts. These had some merit, but there were still extreme stressors and behaviors from children and adults.

Picture trying to clean up a mess while the shit was still hitting the fan. A reasonable person might ask, "Did you turn the fan off?" But I couldn't see the off/on switch. I knew the anxiety and intensity I was experiencing daily and could only imagine that trickled down to my children. I knew there was a disconnect between what I thought should happen and what occurred. I asked for help from a teacher, "My child is having intense meltdowns at home." They responded, "You know mine do too. I'd rather have them do that at home than school." I did not know how to explain what those meltdowns looked like. I did not know the acceptable range of "normal" disruption. Or when speak- ing to the school social worker, I laughed in passing, "Oh, I found him hanging (with his hands) off the blade of his ceiling fan last night!" And she looked at me like I was bizarre and said, "Isn't that dangerous? You should've called the emergency number!" I knew it was dangerous, we had redirected. We removed him from that room, but it had seemed standard for what we were experiencing. I could not figure out how the emergency number would have helped redirect the child. The only people who seemed to "get it" were people who also had to make sure their kitchen knives were covered, kept toothbrushes outside the bathroom so they wouldn't "accidentally" end up in the toilet, and had to reverse the locks on bedroom doors. A family's external chaos will directly impact a child's internal setup. In these families, blaming the loudest problem or disruptive child is easy. It is out of desperation that we do this. When really, we have to start with the caregiver's internal space, then the caregiver's response to the external space, then the response to the child. A caregiver's family history, knowledge, and resistance can block this process.

Professionally, I had worked with children over a decade. Later, I was an interpreter specializing in mental health and legal interpreting. My work has taken me in and out of prisons, drug treatment centers, psych wards, and counseling sessions. I had interpreted through master's degrees in social work, art therapy, and counseling. In my personal life, I have spent extensive time learning the process and theories for inner healing through faith-based approaches. I am no expert, but I had a cache of knowledge and experience in my back pocket. I had grown up with stories about family members with mental diagnoses and knew secondhand the ins and outs of navigating depression, anxiety, bipolar, and schizophrenia, to name a few. The trauma-informed classes through the foster agency were informative. But until you have firsthand experience, the information remains theoretical. I remember vividly, during our adoption interview, the interviewer saying, "Is there any behavior that would cause you to reject these children or request them rehomed?" I confidently answered, "No! Even if someone burned our house down and exhibited such dangerous behaviors that they would need residential placement, they would still be our child and deserve a family to stick it out with them." A few years later, when I discovered a child with a pile of burned matches in my bedroom, my anxiety was on high alert, and my confidence was in ashes. We were naive. Passionate. Clueless.

As I watched my children grow- my stress grew too. Caregiver fears often escalate as our children become more independent because the consequences are often more significant. I was determined not to parent from fear, yet some societal issues are too real. If my 7-year-old Black son runs when his grandma tries to calm him down, what will his 16-year-old response be to a policeman who tells him to "stop"? My child would get so frustrated when someone changes the rules of a game that he blocks them from exiting a room- what will happen to a romantic partner when he is older if he is angry? What if my daughter is in a fight and mentally shuts down when stressed and can't remember what happened? What about the child who hides stacks of cash but has "no memory" of where it came from? Every scenario is a "worst- case" possibility when a child consistently acts unpredictable. This vast ocean of uncertainty can feel like a monster hovering- for the adult and child. Often a child will feel overlooked in their positive behaviors, and the parent will be hyper-vigilant to any "signs" that their child is head- ing down a 'disaster' path.

After many interventions at school with few behavior improve- ments, we decided to homeschool one of our children. In order to track the effectiveness of medication and coping strategies, we needed to find a baseline of behavior, emotions, and identity. Our goal was to remove non-essential stressors to provide the required mental relief to change patterns. I had resisted homeschooling because I didn't know how to help this child. I was stressed being around them. Calm moments were rarely enjoyable, and bonding in these situations was ineffective. Both children and caregivers in cases like this are often experiencing consistently high levels of hyper-vigilance. Constantly flowing cortisol levels and a regressed baseline creates a deficit in all participants. The child may absorb and behave in a way to force rejection. The caregiver feels helpless and puts up walls. Unresolved childhood patterns impact the caregiver's response. The cycle is complex and pain-filled. Instead of having a curious spirit, parents and caregivers rationalize our inability to connect or get on the level of the child we are interacting with. This paradigm overlooks tremendous opportunities to connect.

In the first several months of homeschooling, I had a simple goal: stabilization. [Note: I had taken on the sole responsibility for my family's thriving. A planner by nature, I was setting up as many controls as possible to avoid my own fear of failure and the devastation I may experience. I was sensorily and emotionally overstimulated, and the only way to reduce stimulation was to be over-structured.] My stabilization plan was based on Maslow's hierarchy of needs and modeled through an adoption camp's schedule: meet all physical needs consistently to build a baseline of functioning. Every three hours, we rotated essential needs like eating, rest, gross motor, fine motor, problem-solving, and sensory input. This over- zealous structured approach was out of desperation on my part. I did not win any "success medals"; rather fast-forwarded us on a route of burnout. As the mom, I was the number 1 enemy. Now as teacher, caregiver, disciplinarian, mom, and therapist- I was the main human contact for this child. There was no escaping from each other. I don't recommend this; we were desperate. Years later, when I was able to receive my own diagnosis of C-PTSD and recognize neurodivergent traits, I was able to develop a better vocabulary for asking for help. At the time, my requests for help were overlooked or misinterpreted. Unfortunately, many kids in high-stress, high-isolation settings do not have a way to ask for better support. They do not have the resources to hold adults accountable. For better and worse, this setup is what we chose.

The two of us spent months dancing. The child was determined to dance the foxtrot, and I insisted on the salsa. We danced around control. There was no compromising, and both felt "too much" was at stake. After a while, I finally discovered a somewhat predictable cycle to the child's moods. Week 1 was good. The child wanted to learn and connect. Other than minor behaviors, they could get along with others. Week 2 was an "on edge," scared vibe. The child was very jumpy and could not focus. They still wanted to connect; at least we could read together. They would try to do schoolwork but were very distracted. Week 3 was hell week. The child went to a mental place of numbness, unable to connect. Even if the child did not exhibit dangerous behaviors, there was complete avoidance. You couldn't touch them or be near them. Playing with other kids always produced someone getting hurt or someone going into a rage.

Week 4 was fear week, part two. The child felt scared and remorseful for the prior week. They were still terrified and didn't want to be touched. They couldn't complete any schoolwork. They only wanted media and would simmer because they had not earned the privilege. Every interaction was met with resistance, even though I knew they needed connection and play. During week 4, sometimes I would sit in the same room and repeat, "Buddy, you are ok. You are safe". It felt like brainwashing. What the child mentally experiences is the child's reality. We talked to the doctor about different meds and referrals to behavioral pediatricians or psychologists. We were referred and denied. The other center didn't take the child's insurance, and we'd have to pay $5000 for evaluations. The children's hospital eventually placed us on a 10-month waiting list. While you are dancing with providers and medicines, a child has a simmering invisible need.

An acquaintance had once asked, "Isn't playing with matches just a curious thing? Why would you assume it was something aggressive or dangerous? Why are you assuming the worst?" At the time, there was no way to express the anxiety we experienced. There was a disconnect between cause and effect. There is a difference between the curious play of some children and non-boundaried "curious" play. I needed the same support I was desperately trying to provide for the kids. I needed a safe place to say, "I am terrified every day and don't know how to make that stop". Instead of giving useful strategies, I needed help to grieve. Later I would learn that intellectualization can be a form of dissociation. Reading and research, when done as avoidance, helped me not to feel the emotions and stress in my body. MY desperation was exhibited in the vastness of solutions we pursued. [Note: The children's stress responses often parallel adults' stress responses.] Some parents shut down, and others pursue too many options- either extreme is an SOS flare that may go overlooked. Because we were actively pursuing solutions- it appeared that we, as adults, had it all together- when we were trying to silence the chaos and feelings. We limited sugar and food dyes and allowed sugar and food dyes. We were highly rigid in routine, and we were very laid back. Constantly experimenting to discover the right "life cocktail" kept us hyper-alert to an issue. We rarely let our guard down, allowing our children and our- selves to rest in their current emotional state without fear of behaviors. I had lists of all the developmental growth that had occurred- at that time, this was how I clung to hope. My husband and I had yet to realize how crucial our emotional healing was- so the assumption remained on getting the children help.

I homeschooled two of my children the following year. Diminishing the transitions and stress they struggled with created a more stable emotional experience. However, there were still consistent "substantial behaviors," odd behaviors, and massive meltdowns that would impact everyone in the family. We needed to hone in on a diagnosis or a more specific idea of what the kids were experiencing. We also needed a diagnosis to request school accommodations and support. At the beginning of the summer, I had taken two of our kids in for therapeutic intakes. Two different therapists were assigned to the kids. The seasoned therapist listed her initial thoughts regarding ODD, ADHD, RAD, and anxiety. I had that sinking feeling that what she could offer would mirror the strategies we had used the past two years. She said, "I've seen this situation hundreds of times before. And you generally just have to put up with this until they turn 18". The other therapist completely disregarded the child's dissociative episodes and said kids couldn't have PTSD (Post-Traumatic Stress Disorder).

A few days after those disappointing appointments, my mom sent me Sandra Paulsen's book, "Looking Through the Eyes of Trauma and Dissociation." This book provided vocabulary for what we were seeing! It contained transformational concepts and practices for us. She provided exercises that reinforced what we had already been testing. The case studies could have been written about kids in my home. It was a relief to realize that what we experienced weekly, if not daily, was "dissociation". Dissociation directly impacted my children's ability to function, absorb, and connect. It impacted my ability to meet their needs consistently and fueled precarious frustrations. It also impacted us as caregivers in our own experiences of the world. When we were overwhelmed, we shut down to the emotions and responses- unable to be present in the treasured moments. Identifying an internal "conference table" and learning how to respect and work with those parts was powerful!

Let's press pause in my story and do a check-in. How do you feel as you read this? Have you experienced something similar, or are you thinking of an acquaintance who has expressed similar issues? Notice how your body responds as you read- does it tighten up? Do you feel embarrassed for me? Do you want to rescue the child? Do you feel the urge to share examples from your life? Depending on your reaction, you should read this book slowly- not rushing or forcing. Please journal, take a walk, and continue to check in with yourself through- out the book.

There are also a few terms to become familiar with at this intermission. These will be explained in greater detail later.

Regulated/Dysregulated: Regulation is when our nervous system is stable and can handle the stimuli it experiences. Dysregulation is when our nervous system is on a roller coaster and cannot process the stimuli it experiences. Self-regulation does not necessarily equal calm but is the ability to regulate one's self.

Dissociation/Disassociation: To disconnect from an experience or self to preserve one's safety. To Dis-associate, dis-connect.

Embodiment: An idea "coming alive" in our body- we take on the characteristics that define that concept.

Somatic Awareness: Being aware of our bodily responses and baselines.

Self-states or Parts: A person's internal self may express itself in various ways (age, personality, behavior, etc.).

Neurodivergent: This can include diagnoses like ADHD, Autism (ASD), OCD, and C-PTSD. It refers to a neural (brain) organizational approach different from a "Neurotypical" person.

Conference Table: An activity allowing a person to draw/identify which self-state may respond or make choices.

Trauma: The impact of an event/memory/experience on our bodies and minds.

I believe these concepts are helpful in healing families of origin and intergenerational trauma. I see the positive impact of these principles in working with kids who are neurodivergent and experience a disconnect from their environments. Proactively applying these embodied principles encourages healthy child development regardless of the extreme nature or neutrality of a child's behaviors. Parents who explore their pasts will cultivate environments that help children grow healthy. Instead of placing that responsibility on the child, parents who take ownership of their own internal state will build environments of connection. The external condition of a family directly impacts the internal development of the neural organization of a child. As my spouse and I shifted in our parenting and recognized our own (adult) role in healing, our house became a more stable place for acceptance and growth. This next part of our story highlights the importance of dealing with behaviors and addressing the underlying dissociation experienced by a child and caregiver.

Returning to our story:

Reading Sandra Paulson's book provided tools to use with the kids and me beyond "mindfulness." Please get and read her book- it is a gold mine. The abbreviated concept is to view our brain as a "conference table" (picture a table) with different participants that show up to a meeting. Some people will have more defined participants at this conference table (depending on life experiences, support, and genetic disposition). These participants may have distinctive characteristics that differentiate them from the person's primary personality. For example, if I was very upset, I picture a conference table with participants at a meeting in my mind's eye. Upset Rachel, scared Rachel, adrenaline Rachel, 6-year-old Rachel scared of parent's outburst, etc. Whether drawing this on paper or picturing it in my mind's eye- I can give each "attending the meeting" a chance to voice their concerns, then problem-solve for a more successful interaction. The focus is on internal processing and co-operation of inner parts. This approach can impact external behaviors. I began introducing this concept to a few of the kids - we began to identify different aspects of our internal life and how behaviors shifted depending on who was in charge of the conference table.

A few weeks after we had started becoming comfortable with our internal conference table, one of our other children had his tonsils and adenoids removed. My husband and I stayed with this child at the hospital while trusted grandparents were home with the other four kids. Once we returned home, I was on nurse duty with my recovering kiddo, who had his own sensory processing needs. Dad and grand-parents were managing everything else. A few days later, running on fumes with little sleep, I came out of my room, and the smell of pee hit me in the face. I instantly felt rage flood my body, my thoughts racing, "Of course, when I am at the beck and call of one person who needs me, the desperate needs of this other child will surface. I had spent 8 hours a day for the past year and a half working with this child to help him have stability and security. Why has nothing changed? Why did he not care about anyone else? Why was he so selfish? Why did our lives have to look like this? Why? Why? Why?" [If I were able to articulate it at the time, I would have acknowledged that I felt hopeless, I felt like no other caregiver was competent, I felt sad, I was afraid of other people's responses, I was scared for the future, I was over-stimulated, I didn't know what to do, I wanted to run away, I was sad for him.]

I called this kiddo into their room to find out what was happening- besides the obvious pee aroma everywhere. As the 9-year-old child entered the room, I felt a presence of self-hatred and violence. (To me, this sensation was a heaviness in the air, a sense of claustrophobia, and a panic at being trapped). At that moment, I knew- I had been trying to respond to his "fully functioning 9-year-old self" instead of any other participant at his conference table. This vocabulary of dissociation and mental "conference table" shed light on what we had thought was "unfixable". The child's life experiences had been so disruptive that they experienced a constant barrage from the participants sitting at the conference table. When the child felt danger and fear, these participants would create hazardous or chaotic situations for him. This realization, in real-time, paused any rage and fears flowing from me, and it shifted my view of the ongoing suffering this child was experiencing.

I asked if I could hold the child's hands and sit crisscross facing each other. One purpose of holding hands was bilateral stimulation (activating both sides of the brain by gently squeezing the hands rhythmically back and forth). The second purpose was for the child to have physical touch so they did not have to fear getting hurt (this varies on the trauma history of each person). I asked if I could check in with the child's conference table because it seemed that some internal age was extremely overwhelmed. I sat there and intuitively sifted the internal conference table. I could feel the tension and anger and pictured a sponge that soaked up those overwhelming feelings. Sensing the drowning grief of the child flooded me with compassion. I translated for him what I saw in my mind's eye. "Wow! Your 3-year-old self has some really big feelings! He feels very scared that X was in the hospital. It reminds him of Y in the hospital when you were in a different foster home, and you had no idea what to do without your big sister. That would have felt so scary, huh? What other feelings may a 3-year-old feel about that?" The internal 3-year-old self was showing anger and fear. The 3-year-old self had zero sense of trust for his current age to protect them. The 3-year-old self held all the self-hatred and self-deprecating thoughts. This child could not find stability because his internal self was constantly at war. Heartbreaking. Defeating. But now we had hope.

The child looked at me quizzically because this is not how a "peeing everywhere" incident typically plays out. They started listing a few things a young kid may experience in a fear-filled moment. I validated that the "eldest self" was wise and knew what could help this younger self. We then listened more. The 3-year-old shared how he didn't trust his bigger self to protect him because whenever the 3-year-old made a poor choice, the older self didn't stop him. The child didn't trust him- self and was so angry at himself. I affirmed how big those feelings were and how scary that must feel not to have someone to help put a boundary around you. As I thought about applying this practically, I remembered this child had wanted to learn how to float in the pool. The child's body was constantly in an extremely tense stress state, so he was unable to float. The relaxation strategies we tried didn't matter- the child's body was always too tight to float. I asked the 3-year-old self if they were willing to trust the 9-year-old, not in day-to-day interactions yet, but in the pool. Could the 3-year-old internal self, work with the 9-year-old self to try to float this summer? We would talk more about the anger and memories later, but floating would be something they both enjoyed. Learning to float together would provide positive inter-actions that built their trust and appreciation for each other. It would also give me a measurable way to see if this process was just in my mind's eye or was actually real with concrete applications.

Our summer progressed with good moments and negative hiccups. Running after five kids for seven weeks is busy. We began to "check our conference table" as a routine, so it was not only used in moments of stress. We continued with our routines, daily journals, and sensory experiences. During our last week at the pool, I enjoyed the kids' free-dom. They could all swim in the deep end and do the diving board without me needing to be beside them. I looked up from my book and realized they were all floating. All of them- this child included! They floated from one end of the pool and back. We were just at the beginning stages of this process, but the 3-year-old self felt safe enough with him that it allowed him to float in the pool! The 3-year-old's acceptance of the eldest self-state provided a dramatic decrease in harmful behaviors and a shift in his negative self-talk. I quickly affirmed how wonderful it is to be a team and to feel connected to our parts!

This discovery of an "inner life" was revolutionary for my life, including parenting. I regulated myself closely as I began recognizing how my children's behavior triggered me. My children had the autonomy to develop on their own time-frame, reducing the need for hyper- vigilance and hovering. The big feelings did not diminish, but the sense of helplessness decreased. A few years later, while completing my Master's in Instructional Design, my final project focused on the adult need for supportive environments to process their responses to circumstances. Having a curious and compassionate attitude with a connection to trusted individuals led to intentional decision-making. Shortly after completing my thesis, I learned about NARM (Neural Affective Relational Methods, which focused on curiosity, consent, and connection. This top-down and bottom-up approach focuses on individuals with Complex PTSD. During this training, I was thrilled to discover the overlaps in my academic research and personal experiences with this method.

Throughout this book, we will return to the concept of curiosity, compassion, connection, and cultivation. Choosing to be curious sends our body and mind a message: "Pause! This does not need to be frantic, I can explore different options!" Removing the pressure for immediate response will relieve pressure for yourself and your children. Extending compassion to yourself and your children is a powerful tool. Compassion recognizes we are on the same team, that my struggle is not better or worse than theirs, and that our feelings are valid. Curiosity and compassion help create the space for connection to happen. Without curiosity and compassion, building connections may feel like single-handedly building a bridge over the Grand Canyon. Insur- mountable, frustrating, and exhausting. With curiosity and compas- sion, building the bridge of connection is possible, resulting in cultivation. Cultivating routines, expectations, and self-discipline is effective only from a safe, connected place. The internal life of a child will begin to match the pace of this predictable framework. We cannot always prevent the experiences that cause a starfish child to form- but we can provide safe, connected spaces for them to develop into the fullest version of themselves.

2

Introducing Dissociation

The recent college graduate was busy planning her wedding. Coordinating flowers, outfits, music selections, and a reception- all while living out of state. The bride returned home the week of her wedding with an almost finished to-do list. She had picked a few small tasks for her own mother- walking the delicate tightrope of inclusion and disappointment. The soon-to-be-bride entered her childhood home to a bizarre site. Instead of a wedding cake and flowers covering the kitchen table, her mom had bushels of tomatoes laid out in a canning processional. The galley kitchen connecting the living room to the rest of the house was arrested in a state of epic productivity. The bride asked, "Momma... what's happening?" "Oh, hi Darlin', I'm just canning tomatoes." Some might think the mom was trying to undermine the wedding or be the center of attention. But this level of bizarre was normal. The almost-bride knew this was just how momma had always been. Stable like a roller coaster. Present like unreachable actresses on the television screen. Constant like unpredictable waves.

Humans are multi-faceted. We exist with body, mind, and soul. Our bodies contain muscles, nerves, organs, and bones. Our mind takes the information from our physical body and has systems for processing and storing this information. How our minds interpret these physical stimuli will impact how our brain determines our response. Our soul is our essence, our core, our personality. This "personality" encompasses preferences, values, tendencies, and mood. Our personality will impact our brain, and that will direct our body. For example, a part of my personality is that I am an observer. I watch and take mental notes. My brain knows, based on my history, I will be flooded and feel "unsafe" if someone pressures me to get involved before I have observed. My brain will then signal to my body to respond- I may participate, but my shoulders are tight. Or I may walk away. Or if I trust the person, I will say, "I need time to observe first." Sometimes my "observing" is a protective wall that keeps me isolated; other times "observing" informs me and supports positive connections with others.

Dissociation is to "dis associate" or disconnect internal processing from an external event (whether actual or perceived). Dissociation is a safety strategy our minds use to disconnect our physical body from the overwhelming stress of processing memories and experiences. Picture yourself driving down a road with a roadblock due to a mudslide ahead. The orange barriers and "DO NOT PROCEED" signs direct you to turn around. It is for your safety that you "Do Not Enter!" The barriers are in place to protect during the disaster. At some point, rescue personnel and clean-up crews must "proceed" to attend to the disaster. If they do not proceed, the road will be impassable to any motorists. Trauma is not what happened but the processing of the experience. Dissociation reflects the inability of the "emergency staff" and "clean-up crew" to access the disaster site. The body and mind require a curious space and compassionate pace to reconnect or re-associate. When a person experiences connection within a curious space and compassionate pace, they will expand their capacity to cultivate a new approach. Embodiment "cleans the mudslide" and builds a connection between thought and experience.

It is helpful to use language that supports a multi-faceted mindset. From a young age I was immersed in Christian churches and the concept of good vs. evil was my original framework for a multi-faceted human. Whether you picture an angel and demon on your shoulders or embrace the words of Paul, "I do not understand what I do. For what I want to do, I do not do." The perspective of being "at war against ourselves" led me to polarize my internal experience. If I did good things, I was good. Evil or sin existed within me if I did bad things (or developmentally appropriate kid things). I find the language from NARM (child consciousness and adult consciousness) and the language of IFS for parts work (Managers, Exiles, Firefighters, Self) to provide a better perspective. Using "parts" language can help us improve our understanding of the impacts of trauma on our bodies, mind, and soul. We are not at a grand war with our self. If I reject a challenging or dangerous part of me, I am cutting off all opportunities for that part to receive help. If I accept all of these parts of me, I can provide a safe, boundaried space to encourage connection.

When someone experiences trauma, their mind and body respond with a survival response (fight, flight, fawn, freeze). After the trauma has ended, the person will try to integrate and process the physical, sensory, and emotional information. If the person's body, mind, and soul are able to process the trauma, it will become like a scar (physical or emotional). A scar is still a reminder; a scar may still be sensitive to the touch. This integration depends partially on the person's neural framework, nervous system, "felt safety", age, internal resourcing, and the experience/events.

When someone is unable to integrate the information from a traumatic experience- this contributes to the development of dissociation. This dissociation appears on a spectrum from highly integrated to least integrated. The highly integrated end includes intentional disconnecting and zoning out. Moving toward lesser integration, dissociation can take on five presentations: dissociative amnesia, depersonalization, derealization, identity confusion, and identity alteration. Dissociative symptoms will look and appear different to each person. Dissociative amnesia or fugue is forgetfulness regarding a specific memory or traumatic event. This impacts the ability to trust themselves as they will not know or be aware of their role within certain situations, even if others talk about it. This is not just "forgetfulness" but a protective forgetting that preserves the brains functioning.

Depersonalization is the experience of being "outside of one's body". They may not recognize the person in the mirror, they agree with what is said to "that" person but disconnect that it is themself. This can present as if the person is invisible, they are shocked that people remember them, they over-emphasize acceptance external to their self. Derealization is the experience of the world not being "real" around them. They may experience the world as a distortion (foggy, abstract, sensory sharpness, etc.) or feel like they are watching themself in a movie. They may feel connected to that part but unable to assist or intervene. Identity confusion and identity alteration are when the dissociated parts identify differently. The confusion is a milder form- they may shift age, not recognize their location, and not have a memory of a skill learned. These can connect to the age of a traumatic event. A more robust identity alteration may have different voices, behaviors, and life experiences.

On the least integrated end of the spectrum is structural dissociation which includes identity alteration. This is a person who has at least several different personality identities also known as Dissociative Identity Disorder. Structural dissociation has an ANP (Apparently Normal Part) that handles daily functions and the EP (Emotional Part) that contain elements of the traumatic memories. The ANP is a split from the core personality, but functions as if it were the "face" of the person. People who experienced trauma at young ages may have an ANP they have never been aware of. The ANP can also be known as the "fronting" part. They may not know their "core" self because the ANP has directed their ability to exist. The relationship between the EPs and the ANP determines several types of structural dissociation. Some people will experience an ANP with several EPs- these EPs may trust the ANP and have a somewhat cohesive interaction. Some people will experience EPs that are not understood or disconnected from the ANP. These EPs may experience such desperation that they act out in self-harming or highly disruptive ways. And the most intense form is with individuals who have experienced traumas that result in several or more ANPs each having additional EPs. These ANPs will have different ways of functioning and interacting in their environment. These multiple personalities may be obvious to the person and those around them.

This book's focus is childhood dissociation. A child who experienced trauma, did not have the support to process and integrate their ANP or fronting parts, will grow into an adult with structural dissociation. The child could experience dissociative amnesia, depersonalization or derealization during childhood but it becomes more rigid as they age. At its extreme presentation, an adult may have numerous internal identities that have rigid boundaries. These different identities hold different memories, behaviors, and thought patterns. The adult may or may not realize they exist this way. Though there is some research about children's experiences with dissociation, it is hard to analyze what is intangible. It is my thought that children, while still developing, have a more flexible dissociative framework. The ANPs and EPs formed from trauma may still have the potential to be integrated as the child grows up. Due to the massive rewiring in teenage years, the internal family of a child may experience numerous opportunities for integration. Accurately identifying a child's dissociative tendencies will empower their self-connection and encourage integration. If we overlook the child's internal selves, and their needs for development and support, we neglect to take care of the whole child. The internal selves of a child will continue in disruption and stress if I only teach the eldest age of the child positive coping skills. Teenagers will be unaccountable for their choices if they exist in a multi-faceted personality. A caretaker part will try to show responsibility, but other parts will sabotage efforts due to their unresolved pain. How we respond to children and teenagers will impact the integration and acceptance of their inner selves.

Dissociative strategies are strategies that perpetuate disconnect. These create a backlog of processing, which in turn impact the neural functioning of a person. "Be present" requires a connection between this moment and what I am experiencing. If I have a backlog of disconnected stimuli, my brain will be unable to "be present". Connective strategies will encourage curious spaces at a compassionate pace. This support allows children and adults to cultivate an intentional response the next time they encounter the same stimuli. For example, yelling is generally a dissociative strategy. It is not an invitation to "do better". However, there are times when a parent may yell to keep their child out of danger or even when the parent loses it. If the caregiver follows up with a connective strategy- the child will then understand, "Dad isn't upset my ball went in the street; he was scared for my safety". Or "sometimes people, adults and children, lose it- and then repair by apologizing." Connective strategies will invite connection.

Embodied disconnection is when we may disconnect on purpose. If I am overwhelmed with the sounds of my kids playing video games, I will intentionally go to another room, put headphones on, or "tune out" the voices and sounds. I am intentionally disconnecting from the experience because I am overwhelmed or annoyed at the sounds. Embodiment is when we recognize a feeling or sensation in our bodies and decide or have a reflex in response to that sensation. Minor dissociation (more integration) is a disconnect between my feelings and actions. If I do not recognize my sensory overwhelm by the sounds, begin to get irate, and start yelling at my kids to pick up their toys- I do not recognize the connection between the sounds and my discomfort, which impacts my response. Moderate dissociation is a disconnect between what is currently happening and what has happened in my past. If my parent beat me when I got loud, I may have an "inner child" prompt to silence my children for their safety. As I feel my anxiety and feeling of nonsafety rising, the irritation at my children's sounds may increase. I may yell at them to be quiet, frantically start taking their tablets from them, and be angry that they are not listening. "Do they not feel the upcoming danger?" This can be a C-PTSD response from someone who lived with ongoing stressors that impacted their development and ability to respond appropriately. There is a disconnect be- tween the sound of the children, my choice, and the impact of the angry parent figure from childhood. Major dissociation is when the person's system switches to a differently defined personality/identity. This could appear differently based on the identity of the self if the noises of the children are too great, the adult "senses" impending danger, and then switches identity. If it is a "caregiver" persona, the self may swoop in to care for the children. If it is an angrier identity, some- one could be harmed. It may not be evident from an external perspective that an internal shift has occurred.

Putting myself in the child's perspective- if I am happily playing video games and see my mom put in earbuds, I may or may not con- nect parental behavior with the sounds of my game. If my caregiver has discussed ways to set a "noise boundary", I may notice they set it by wearing headphones. Children learn self-regulation from co-regulating with their caregivers. However, if I am happily playing video games and my mom starts yelling at me- my brain will shift from enjoyment into guarded mode. "Why is Mom yelling at me? What did I do?" Suppose this happens consistently without the caregiver clarifying, "Wow, some- times those game noises drive me crazy and I need to find a way to help myself." The child will develop a disorganized neural response because the cause and effect are unclear. The child may tune out whenever the parent yells at them or become hyper-vigilant and begin "predicting" the parent's discomfort before it occurs. The yelling is not an invitation to make a different choice. The interaction does not accurately put the responsibility on the parent's sensory needs. The child will respond defensively or shut down without a clear way to resolve the situation. After releasing that energy build-up, the parent feels better and contin- ues their day as if nothing happened. If this is a constant pattern of interaction within a house, the child may never connect the dis- comfort source with the parent's aggression. The child may use video games to hide when being yelled at. The parent may view the child's playtime as a constant annoyance. An adult's internal experience will impact their external response. This may look like the parent demanding a behavior shift in the child to reduce parental distress. A dissociated interaction will leave both the parent and child confused and shut down- carrying blame with no clear path of change. A connected interaction would involve the caregiver recognizing their feeling and source of irritation and recognizing the impact on the child- then handling it in a way that respects both parties.

For individuals who have experienced sexual, physical, verbal, and emotional traumas, the brain dissociates from the moment of pain and intensity as a form of self-preservation. This preservation is good. This is not weak or a convenient escape - the brain chose to salvage as much of "us" as possible within these safe havens. Dissociation is one of the most extreme strategies of the body/mind to preserve our self. Exposure to some of these one-time or ongoing traumas can devastate a human's system. It is incredible to think that even at our most defenseless, our self preserved as much of "us" as possible. While our mind created a safer internal neural space- unfortunately, our bodies will still experience what has occurred. Nerves, muscles, and bones all hold cellular and fiber memories of the physical impact of these traumas. For example, if I stub my toe walking in my kitchen, I will remember: "Wow, my toe is still throbbing because I stubbed it earlier today." If I stubbed my toe while being screamed at and chased, I may have no memory of that encounter. I just know that my toe hurts really bad, the toenail looks bruised, and I feel "wonky" because I do not remember when/how it happened. As a child, if I already lived in an environment with inconsistent connection, these dissociative moments feed into my ongoing development of self. I may feel paranoid about the "lost memories" that cause me continual harm. I may feel I have no control over my life and daily interactions.

Unfortunately, individuals experiencing these ongoing atrocities are often within the care of caregivers who experienced and passed down similar pains. As a child is still hitting critical developmental milestones, these internal safe spaces will often connect to a certain chronological age for that child. This creates a developing child with internal selves that may develop at varied paces while appearing externally to be their "oldest" age self. These internal parts tend to be separate from each other unless intentional trust and compassion work occurs to help integrate them. Using the starfish example, picture a child as a starfish who has ongoing "severing"- traumas that impact neural processing. For each "severing", a new starfish begins to grow. The child has their original starfish, albeit missing a leg. The next starfish has a leg and a few organs but is developing more parts. Another leg gets severed, so more development begins on this new starfish beginning. This motley starfish crew is viewed as one "being"- expected to function at the developmental age of the original starfish. If the environment continues to be hostile for the starfish, some "developing" starfish will die out; others will experience more severing. We would not shame a starfish for falling apart and ceasing to function - we look for environmental impacts, a shift in the gene structure, etc. However, when a child, composed of many developing parts, is falling apart- we often shame them for not developing as expected.

A child living in a trauma environment must maintain these separate states in order to survive. They are not in Post-Trauma; they are still in protection mode. Their ANP or fronting part will maintain their daily functions. Each distinct developmental age and/or EPs may appear at different times throughout the child's day, which causes additional struggles for the child. Children are curious, and self-states are no different. A child presenting externally as a 10-year-old will experience frustrations and consequences during a school day if their 3-year-old self takes over the frontal lobe steering wheel. The 3-year-old internalizes an additional message of shame based on their age behaviors not fitting the environment. The physical body of the 10-year-old experiences muscle tightness, a stomach in knots, a foggy head, and fatigue from over-excitement during the day. This child then receives a negative note to take home, but at that stage, the body is eager to disconnect from the confusion and pain anyway, regardless of parental response. Dissociative strategies will only encourage further disconnect for this developing human. This is why a curious space and compassionate pace are essential for supporting the ongoing development of a multi-faceted child.

Development of Dissociation:

Various factors can impact the development and degree of dissociation, such as an individual's neural framework, nervous system, "felt safety" of the individual, age, internal resourcing, and the experience/event.

Neural framework impacts dissociation and dissociative tendencies. Nerves send signals, wait for a response, and build a neural pathway in the direction of the response. Picture a frequently walked path in a forest- branches cleared and a walking path stamped down by many hikers. Or visualize a deer path - the grassy trail diagonal through the woods used by many animals to create a smaller, well-traversed path. These frequently traveled paths require less effort to walk. An infrequently walked path will require more effort to hike - the ground covered with vines or tall grass, branches covering the trail. Frequently experienced neural pathways are more entrenched - you can picture a deeper groove in a path, a thicker cord, or a sturdy bridge. It is not just "more comfortable," but our impulse will follow the path of least resistance. A less traveled neural path will require more energy to travel down-picture a forest path covered with plants, a thinner cord, or a wobbly bridge. Some children's neural impulse is to travel the "road less traveled". Explored further in the next chapter, a neurotypical child's brain pathway will follow different pathway patterns than a neurodivergent child's neural pathways. For all humans, these pathways are built heavily during our earliest years of childhood. At age 13, the brain has reached maximum size but undergoes intense remodeling. During the teenage years, the brain experiences pruning and re-solidifying pathways until age 25. Adult brains can develop new pathways and responses - it just will take longer. Unprocessed childhood traumas and dissociation in adults require intentional work to connect their experiences. Suppose a child who has experienced trauma and dissociation was supported with curious spaces and compassionate pacing. In that case, their "emergency clean-up crew" will have support in returning to the mental disaster site.

Our nervous systems connect our brain and body. The CNS (Central Nervous System) handles communication from our brain and spinal cord. The PNS (Peripheral Nervous System) relays the rest of the information (cranial, autonomic, nerves, etc.) to the central nervous system. The SNS (Somatic Nervous System) and the ANS (Autonomic Nervous System) are within the PNS. The Somatic system relays information from our skin, muscles, and joints. The Autonomic system handles a variety of involuntary motor control functions. On a basic level - if our body experiences "felt safety," it will relay a message to our brain "I am safe, I can feel relaxed, I am not on guard." This will impact the speed of our brain, heart rate, or ability to process extra information. If our body feels unsafe, it will send that message to the brain. If the brain determines we are in danger, we may enter "fight or flight". If the brain interprets the interaction as life-threatening, we may progress into "freeze" or "fawn"- dissociation, depression, and hopelessness occur in this range. A child may internally experience the ANP in a calm, vagal state but the EP in a sympathetic state (fight or flight). Recognizing dissociation will impact our response. If a child has experienced numerous experiences of starvation- their neural pathway will recognize a missed meal as "a threat to existence". Even if they have had stable food for years, their EP could be on high alert if food is not present. A child who has food stability and then misses a meal, their neural pathway may recognize this as a "potential danger," and they become "hangry" as a signal that they need food. But the brain will not recognize the missed meal as a threat to their survival.

The Dorsal Vagal State is when the system cannot protect itself, cannot respond, and will shut down. For example, someone who falls into the fetal position while being attacked or cooperates with the attacker while unaware of their surroundings. They are "numb" and going through the motions but unable to respond. "Post-trauma", the "clean-up crew's" inability to process the experience can cause dissociation from a slowed dorsal state. In an example where someone is attacked and fights off their attacker, but post-trauma they did not receive support to process. They may internalize shame, have a flood of memories, and have a surge of somatic energy, which may overload their system, causing them to enter freeze. This unresolved trauma continues to play out throughout their life if it does not receive the compassionate connection needed. We cannot live in a constant freeze state. This is when our mind "preserves" and forms an ANP to guide our functioning.

"Felt sense of safety" impacts the child's ongoing development of dissociation. This is not the question "Is the child safe" but rather "Does the child embody safety?" Embodiment takes the concept of "love", "safety", and "support" from an idea into a felt emotion and physical sensation. This will often require us to slow down our interactions to make space for our bodies to feel - whether it is laughter, sadness, anger, or curiosity. "Safety" is not just a word but a state of being within our bodies that exudes calm, presence, and security. For example, a spouse that says, "My partner loves me so much," yet their demeanor shifts whenever that partner is around may not feel an embodied experience of love and connection. A child in a "safe" space yet disembodied will be unable to settle, stop scanning the room, or control the environment. The "felt safety" will reflect which nervous system state the child is experiencing. Laurence Keller's Neuro Affective Relational Model, suggests the approach of 50/50, where we are 50% attuned to our own embodied experience and 50% attuned to our environment or other individuals around us. A child who has learned to manage the adults around them will be highly attuned to external responses. They are then highly disconnected from their own experience. A child who is 80% attuned to the caregiver interactions and 20% to their own response will feel unheard and overlooked. An ANP who is keeping the child surviving, will often ignore the EP due to the intensity of their pain. The ANP who ignores the EP and hyper-fixates on the adult's behavior will experience high distress. The behaviors can fuel a volatile cycle between the EP needing help, the ANP trying to manage survival, and the adult trying to manage behaviors.

The age of trauma(s) impacts the child's development due to dissociation. Experiences in utero and pre-verbal years will store in a different part of the brain than memories connected to expressive language. (A 1-year-old's memory will connect through senses, whereas a 10-year-olds memory will include verbal or expressed language.) Trauma impacts developmental milestones. Remember- if the inner "emergency crew" cannot return for clean-up, the "road" will continue to be blocked. Some children will develop detours around the "neural mudslide" - these survival strategies will eventually show up in ways caregivers see as misbehavior. If a child is in an environment where they experience ongoing traumas- they may have developmental blocks at various skills and ages. For example, if a 9-year-old experienced ongoing trauma at 8-months-old, the 9-year-old may not have developed object permanence. Their separation anxiety could be stunted and not look "age appropriate". The neural "emergency workers" will continue to block the mental site if the child is punished for their "inability to be alone". If the child is safely encouraged to practice object permanence and practice a caregiver coming and going- the neural "emergency workers" may begin to allow access to the site of woundedness.

An adult who experienced a childhood full of traumas without support to process will often be a jumble of varying internal ages - and they will not know it! We do not see that it is "odd" because it is very real to us. In their adult years, they may see a disconnect between how they relate to the world and what exists in their brains/bodies. Children living in dissociative environments will develop neural pathways prone to dissociative strategies. Children living with dissociation at specific ages will develop an "internal family". By their upper teenage years, these developed internal "individuals" are vying for safety and support. If a caregiver is unaware, they will focus on a child's chronological age, not the child's developmental or "at the age of trauma" age.

An individual's internal resourcing impacts the development of dissociation. The "emergency clean-up crew" is your internal resource crew! They can not prevent trauma and hard things from happening.

Still, it is their responsibility to create a parameter around a disaster zone, inform other parts of the danger, clean up, and recognize cues to avoid a further disaster potentially. An adult with dissociative strategies is a previous child taught dissociative strategies by their own caregiver. Post-trauma, this adult's internal "clean-up crew" cannot recognize cues about further danger. They may give off a constant warning, "danger ahead", even if the threat has subsided. There will also be a backlog of processing- which causes overtaxing our brain and body with stress. Imagine the mudslide stacked on top of 10 years of mudslides - multiple layers need to be processed to "reopen" the road. If the adult tries to experience sadness or loneliness, the internal "clean-up crew" may shut down vulnerable feelings, and the adult does not feel like they can trust themself. An adult raised with connective, embodied strategies will feel emotions, trust their internal process to "clean-up," and reconnect when appropriate. They will be able to be "present" due to not having a system backlog.

A child's development of internal resourcing requires self-trust. It is essential for the child's internal world to feel safe, especially for a child who experiences a dissociative disconnect. The EP is learning to trust and connect with the ANP. They can develop a relationship that says, "I will work in our best interest!" Kids who experience trauma will often blame themself. The internal system will look alienated- internal parts vying for attachment and survival. If I, as the adult, try to force the child to connect with me- they will experience a heightened conflict within themself. I can model and encourage self-trust and safe spaces, but I want to promote self-connection. It is almost like we can "mentor" the ANP to become a safe grounding space for the EPs. This self-trust leads to wise decision-making, self-care, and connecting to others.

Children who have experienced trauma, dissociate in order to survive, and then are forced into behavioral expectations will often not receive the ongoing developmental care to encourage their dissociations to integrate with the rest of themself. These children grow into adults with more solidified dissociative experiences - often hidden, held as "secrets" within the body and mind. Secrets perpetuate shame, and shame prevents holistic growth. Often these children have been expressing their need for safety, compassion, and healing for years- and those behaviors usually repel instead of invite healing relationships. When they feel safe, our Beings (body, mind, soul) always extend the invitation to healing. A child who lives within the environment of on- going trauma is in the situation of their Being trying to resolve the dissociations, yet needing to maintain survival or safety. A child who moves into a new home often continues to experience the need for survival- either due to the trauma of separation from the family of origin or the environment of the new family placement. Children with a diagnosis may experience the on-going little "t" traumas stemming from undiagnosed parents' behaviors and emotional needs. They may also experience the constant stressors of masking, of being told to silence their stemming behaviors and sensory needs- which can be physically silenced or shame-silenced. Creating safe spaces is the baseline.

3

Case Study

Much of the work surrounding dissociation involves theories and anecdotal experiences. Research frameworks are limited in their scientific approach due to the number of variables. With an adult who experiences dissociation, there is a process of realizing, "Wait, is this not how other people experience the world?" And then learning to recognize your own responses, triggers, memories, and situations that impacted your dissociation. You may be able to look back and pinpoint key traumas where a split occurred. For other people, their life has been lived at a "dual" level, assuming living a "double life" (engaged and disengaged) is typical. This is an ongoing experience connected with C-PTSD. For children, who are still in the midst of developing their bodies, minds, and psyches - it is more difficult to recognize a split self-state. The following is a summary of a dissociative child based on a conglomeration of experiences.

Child, age 8. Experienced various forms of abuse and neglect. Her internal self contains several ages and personas that reflect ages of trauma and areas of need. This child will jump between ages depending on their level of overwhelm. Sometimes developmentally, she will reflect a toddler, other times a 5-year-old. Other times she seems like an adult. This is reflected in her sensory input, her posturing, responses, and cues for comfort. She also has "internal personas" including "the spy/the eye", the bully, the memory holder, the auntie, and obsessions.

The rupture of self during trauma created the beginning of a persona, or an ANP (Apparently Normal Personality) and then EP (Emotional Personality) that represent different responses to the trauma. Each EP can represent somatic, sensory, emotional, and peripheral responses to the trauma. Because this child's traumas were severe and consistent from an early age, there is not a distinction between her "fronting self" and her core self. Hyperactivity and mood swings are viewed as pre-puberty shifts - instead of internal states needing stabilization. Ongoing friendship issues are viewed as "normal" for 4th grade girls.

Example: The child was frequently left outside in the cold with no access to a caregiver, food, or housing when they were younger. The child, unable to care for themselves, will mentally "retreat" to a safe space. The ANP forms to preserve the child's mental, physical and emotional safety. The ANP may direct the child to beg for food, hide under a bench, or walk into a store. EP's may form connected to hunger (food stability and comfort), loneliness (distrust of others, potential distrust of self), temperature (either allergic to cold or numb to the cold). If the ANP acts in the best interest of the child- finds a helpful authority figure who provides food and shelter, and finds the caregivers - the EP's will be sensitive to hunger, cold, loneliness- but will trust the ANP to work in their best interest. The ANP may protect the child, but in a way that harms the child. An example is the ANP guiding the child to ask the first stranger they see for help, the stranger takes them to an unsafe place. Or the ANP directs the child into a store, the child steals some food because they are hungry, the child gets chased or in trouble for the theft. The EP will resist the ANP's provision in the future. The hunger EP may be aggressive or pushback at any provision by the ANP. Internally the EP will look for their own companions for loneliness, in-stead of trusting the ANP's relationships. Externally, this may look like a child unable to maintain friendships or sabotaging the relationships they are in.

The resistance of the EP's can be tied to the resistance of the en-vironment, support system, and levels of understanding. A child living with internal discord, in an environment constantly questioning and challenging their cohesion, will experience inner parts that "dig in their heels" to feedback, because the inner parts are concerned with survival. Each individual part sees their job as "preserving" the child - whether in positive or negative ways. Cohesion requires trust with the child or an ANP that is trustworthy and works in the child's best interest. Children with internal discord, reinforced in their environment by disconnect, will grow into adults with dissociated structural dissociation or heavily dissociated realities. If a child can be provided with support to integrate their aspects, in a low threatening environment there will be a cohesion of internal parts. This may mean integration of semi-splits back into the whole, this may mean a conscious awareness of various parts and a compassionate unity between this internal "family".

Once this child reaches their teenage years their mind is pruning neural pathways. It is as if all areas of traumas open their doors slightly, peeking out to see "Is now the time to show myself?" To a child with an already jumbled internal state, these appearances can feel alarming and dangerous. Overlooked self-states ooze pain and will bring attention to their need in any means necessary. The adolescent's fronting state or ANP has been guiding this child for years. It is exhausted. The ANP was intended to protect within the moment of need, not to be an ongoing guide for the teenager during high school or comforter for the internal younger ages still reeling from trauma memories. The teenager then vacillates between steady and chaotic, kind and hateful. Self-harm and self-sabotaging behaviors begin. Exhaustion and low-verbal states occur. "But aren't all teenagers moody and distant? Don't all teenagers experiment with harmful behaviors and the redirect over time?" All teenagers experience a grand rewiring of the brain. All teenagers experience a decades long practice of developing and becoming independent.

Teenagers and young adults who experienced trauma in younger years and dissociative strategies will be "revisiting" these memories and experiences. Their brains will be testing dissociative strategies and connective strategies. Their rapidly growing bodies will be assessing the muscular and cellular memories of trauma - if unprocessed, these get stored only to resurface later as mysterious symptoms. Traumatized or not, all teenagers benefit from reflections on their childhood stories and affirmation of connective relationships. Teenagers who experienced trauma need help organizing their internal parts. They need safe support to address the conflict of helplessness with independence, self-preservation and defensiveness, acceptance of self while reassessing the fronting part. Depression, anxiety, bipolar, ADHD, ODD- there are many diagnoses for teenagers that would improve with a reflection on the trauma history and potential parts of a child. The fronting part may display behaviors indicative of ODD, but inner EPs or child parts will be penalized and suppressed by the strategies. ADHD meds may help the exhausted fronting part organize and "perform" better in daily functions, but the inner parts asking for help will be silenced and ignored. Mindfulness will only benefit the presenting part and can re-trigger other self-states. Teenage years are full of opportunities for self-connection, if the child's environment encourages compassion, curiosity, and connection. The teenager and their internal parts can cultivate a beneficial pathway. A teenager who experiences dissociation through derealization and/or depersonalization will experience a growing rift between their younger self and older parts. This "numbness" contributes to self-harm, self-destructive choices, unstable ego, and an inability to be held accountable.

Teenagers who have experienced connective environments may begin to experience physical symptoms. These physical symptoms of variety of illnesses are often how trauma metabolizes through the body. A child receiving support may finally feel an inner relief. Inner parts that were clenched, holding to stored memories, releases their grip. This "release" is positive but initially can cause havoc on a body as the physical system tries to re-regulate itself. Teenagers who lived in the "freeze" state of the nervous system may experience their bodies shifting into fight/flight. This trajectory is positive - because the nervous system is 'waking up' and moving towards a regulated existence. The behaviors can be extremely dangerous and disruptive. The teenager may experience the need to run (they were unable to runaway from abuse as a child), they may fight (they were unable to defend themself as a child), they may speak aggressively (they were unable to advocate for their needs when younger). Viewing these disruptions as a "negative trajectory" can send the child back into freeze and dissociative states. Allowing the teenager to express grief and anger towards all they experienced, allows them to shift closer to a regulated, connected human existence. As the child receives support and nurturing of all their disparate parts, the self begins to collect its puzzle pieces. These puzzle pieces help the child to formulate their story and have control of their healing path.

4

Impacts of Dissociation

Children who have experienced traumas from an early age may be living in functional dissociation. Parents who focus on the child's chronological age may miss the opportunity to support the development and connection between ANP and other dissociative parts. This chapter will introduce the impact of dissociation on the development of neural organization, treatment efficacy, and intergenerational traumas. "Potential Indicators of Dissociation" are contained in the book's resource section. If this concept is new to you and you are trying to understand how it appears in tangible examples - look through some of the indicators. If you feel this information applies to you as the caregiver, there are helpful books and resources for adults with dissociation.

-Development of Neural Organization

On a basic level, neural organization is how our brain processes stimuli or information. This information is absorbed through our senses (sight, touch, balance, etc.) and then translated and stored neurally. Our brain's processing and storing procedures directly impact the processing of traumas and positive experiences. Recall the forest path picture-information travels on cleared or crowded neural pathways. How information is processed impacts behavior.

"Neurotypical" refers to a "typical" way the brain processes information. It may follow paths and neural connections traditionally viewed as a "top-down" perspective. Our brain absorbs sensory data, looks for previous knowledge, and then draws an inference and action choice based on this information. An example is a friend who ignores me in the hallway. My prior knowledge is this person is my friend, and we have not had an argument; I assume they are not angry at me, and I choose to ask them if they are having a hard day. If a neurotypical child experiences dissociative strategies from their parents ("Stop crying, you are such a baby!"), the child will have the previous knowledge, "My care-giver does not like it when I cry." This child may proactively wipe away tears and hide their crying based on the previous knowledge of a parent's reluctance to comfort. The child will learn to silence or dissociate from their feelings around their caregiver. The predictable pattern allows the child to build a predictable defense.

"Neurodivergence" refers to how these stimuli follow neural paths and connections in a divergent way. Frequently experienced as "bottom-up" thinking- the individual experiences various sensory inputs, the brain pieces these together and attaches an emotion, then draws a conclusion not necessarily based on previous knowledge. Based on the previous friend example - I wave at my friend in the loud hallway, my friend ignores me, and someone bumps into me, spilling my books; I look up, my friend is gone, and I feel loneliness and sad-anger. My brain translates this input into: "My friend is angry at me and refused to help when I dropped my books." This is the path the neural connections follow. The person is probably not consciously thinking, "I have a hor-rible friend". Rather their brain makes these assessments within several seconds. Then throughout the day, the brain cycles back and repeats, "My friend doesn't like me. I am lonely," reinforcing the belief. Because the brain does not use previous knowledge as a baseline, neurodivergent people often crave predictability and routine, as it decreases our stress and the energy required to function. If a neurodivergent child experi-ences dissociative strategies from their parents, the child will not have a cause-and-effect connection. The amygdala will frantically be on guard for danger- not understanding cues and patterns. The child's brain will work overtime, seeking patterns and predictability. Over time, this processing causes a stressed brain and body to be hyperactive, unable to focus, and often dissociated from the cause-and-effect stimuli.

Neurodivergent individuals have an over-connection of neurons the brain. If the "typical" person has 50-75% connection of neurons, neurodivergent individuals will have 75-85% connectivity. A study in 2011 from Courchesne, Mouton, et al, found 67% more neurons in the prefrontal cortex of Autistic children than non Autistic children. These additional connections lead to more neural pathways options, the extra energy required for processing, and non-typical routes of connection. As the brain develops, it experiences a pruning process. In a neurotypical brain, the neural connections will be pruned based on non-usage. Neurodivergent brains experience pruning less predictably and often retain more synapses than a neurotypical brain. The clash between neurotypical expectations and neurodivergent organization often leads to children absorbing dissociative strategies. This leads to lifelong dissociation patterns- in social spaces, with family, at school, in situations of responsibility, and in extracurricular activities. Embodied and connective strategies enable these pattern-masters to connect with themself, advocate for themself, and thrive within various settings.

Neurotypical compared to neurodivergent may also be visualized as comparing a 2D movie with a 4D movie experience. Our zoo had a 4-D Dora the Explorer movie in the children's section. As the film played, the seats would rumble, and water would occasionally mist down. What was fun for one child felt scary for another. A 2D experience would involve watching and ingesting the information, having feelings, and walking away from the theater at the end. A 4D experience involves watching, ingesting information, processing sensory input, and walking away with potentially wet clothes. Imagine entering a traditional 2D movie theater - picture yourself sitting in traditional in theater seats, the lights dim, and you settle in to watch a classic, Penguins of Madagascar. What would you experience? What senses are activated? Do you enjoy or like this movie? Now picture yourself running into a friend after the movies. Your friend says, "That was the worst movie experience I had! It was too intense, and there was too much going on!" From your 2D movie lens, you may think they are being dramatic, or something is wrong with them. If you knew they had watched the 4D version- you would expand your understanding of their experience. They sat down to watch the movie, their seats shook during fight scenes, confetti dropped from the ceiling, and a person in a penguin costume walked through the theater at one point. You sat down and watched a movie in a still seat, with no confetti or penguin costumes. One is not better than the other- it is just a different experience.

This understanding is essential in using connective, embodied strategies while working with children who are neurodivergent. ADHD, ASD, OCD, Dyslexia, Dyscalculia, and Complex-PTSD are a few labels under neurodivergence. Continually processing information and stimuli causes neural pathways to follow various paths that may seem unpredictable to someone outside of that body. The caregiver/ adult response directly impacts the child's continual development of neural connections. When we punish children due to their brains following a different pathway, we teach them to distrust their bodies and minds and rely only on external feedback. Using dissociative strategies (consequences with no connection to an event, shaming, physical punishment, placing caregiver emotions on the child) causes a child to retreat into an internal safe space. When these "refuge" events occur, a child is pressing pause at their current developmental state to maintain the energy required to exist. We cannot skip developmental stages, so a child will pickup from where they paused. Imagine watching a 2-hour movie, pausing it every 15 minutes for 20 minutes; you will drastically lengthen the movie's time. Children exposed to continual stimuli that encourage dissociation will experience developmental stages extended beyond the expected time. Often these children will experience additional shaming or punishment for not being "at the right stage", which can exacerbate their development. Children who experience asynchronous development already experience pressures to "catch up" or perform within a system not based on their individual development. Connective strategies allow these children to develop at their pace, with the proper support needed. Dissociative processes attempt to rush or punish children for a brain not functioning at the pace of external deciders.

One day a teacher called to say she had caught my 3rd grader cheating on a test. The teacher was confused because she had seen the child complete the test from across the room- he was often the first done with 100% accuracy. She watched him erase his test, lean over to another student and copy their answers. The new answers were mostly wrong. She was confused at the 'why' behind his actions. The best answer I could give was that this child trusts the environmental cues more than their internal "knowing". If everyone else was still working on it, surely he was wrong because he didn't fit the pattern. Life experience had taught him to distrust his inner knowing and be hyper- aware of environmental cues. Reminding him of "no cheating" may deter the behavior but not address the impulse. Penalizing the cheating could become a control issue because he didn't remember doing it. Here is an example from home from this same child who is now in 7th grade. Yesterday, they were going to shower (beforehand, he has a mental checklist to collect a towel, washcloth, and lotion). I heard the door open and water running, the child had decided to brush his teeth and pick out the right belt. It did not follow the path my brain said to follow. The child's brain followed the action path that made sense to them. Due to neural processing differences, daily interactions can be a huge source of family conflicts. The goals of the caregiver and child often collide. If I remember that I am parenting from a bottom-up perspective that factors in dissociation - my reaction will focus on the child's entire existence, not just my confusion or irritation.

If an individual's body is using large portions of energy to focus on one task - they will be unable to complete other tasks efficiently. It appears as a lack of compliance, apathy, or manipulation from the outside. One example is group work within the classroom: if a child is using so much brain power to handle the social interaction, understand who is in charge, navigate the transitions, sensory inputs, and any other factors - they may be unable to use additional mental energy to complete the work. Tiering expectations will radically change group interactions. Adults and caregivers must decide if the goal is to complete the work or to work as a team. The adult could choose to assign roles within a group, reducing one component of neural focus. The adult could set the goal as "5 minutes of discussion with three different viewpoints" and shift the goal away from a completed assignment and instead focus on peers navigating a social interaction without arguing. If the adult ascertains that group work is a requirement, there is no shift in approach, and there will be a consequence if not completed - the child will not gain the skills necessary to navigate this situation successfully. The child's brain will decide which item to focus on- often, this will appear as micromanaging others, sharpening pencils repeatedly, telling jokes/not contributing. A neurotypical child with "top-down" thinking may remember- in group work, one person takes notes, gives ideas, and turns in one paper. A neurodivergent child with "bottom-up" processing may feel irritated at the group placement. Their sensory experience of outrage rises, and their brain conserves energy by shutting down processing. The child sits there angry, getting more annoyed by the group conversation, and feels the teacher assigned this group maliciously. Their conclusion is - the teacher doesn't like me, I am not good at group work, and now I am in trouble. (Remember, this may be the child or maybe the child's ANP and EP responding to the situation). Incremental goals/expectations provide the child to develop self-awareness and connection, which enable successful interactions and reflections.

Understanding neural development and human development is vital for cultivating curiosity and compassion. When a caregiver is curious and compassionate, they extend connection and safety to themself and the child. If the caregiver can recognize their contribution to dissociative strategies they will be able to address their own inner healing and cultivate a safe developmental environment for the child. Often caregivers who are at max capacity will have experienced a history of dissociative strategies used on them. Caregivers who choose to address their history and their own experiences will have a dramatic impact on the lives around them. Let us look at the effect of dissociation on treatment efficacy.

-Treatment Efficacy

Picture the internal self as a puzzle. Over time, we gain puzzle pieces for new developmental ages, skills, and core memories. Your puzzle pieces will cover different senses, emotions, and body movements. Part of being human is constructing a story of where you fit in the world and how you connect within your environment. Sometimes you may feel like your pieces are jumbled or not put together. There may be times when you can't find the right piece. Now imagine that some of those pieces are put away into a lockbox to avoid getting lost. This lockbox is not an intentional resistance to change. Instead, it is a protective stance of the mind - to protect the entire body from additional stress. As our Being (body, mind, soul) attempts to unify itself, the lockbox retains the pieces, and the puzzle remains unfinished. Some of these pieces in the lockbox will become agitated and aggressive, trying to communicate their need to get out. Some pieces go further into shutdown depressive states at the lack of self-connection. One of the risks of ignoring dissociation is that individuals will experience on- going treatment, therapy, and support focused on external behaviors without getting the root-help they need. One of the risks of ignoring dissociation and dissociative strategies in children is that the caregivers are often direct contributors to their child's dissociative experience. The caregiver expects the child to function in a way that benefits the family unit or school environment, even with puzzle pieces stuck in the lockbox. Finding the appropriate mode of therapy is essential in cultivating a safe internal environment for a child and a secure external environment for the family.

Let's step back from dissociation for a minute. Picture this scenario and reflect on the variables in this situation: your child sprained their ankle and needs rehab to gain strength in the leg. A gap exists between expectation (running, playing) and performance (the child can only hobble and still has pain). The parent first assesses the issue and determines if they can handle it or need an expert opinion. They may have a preferred doctor or have resistance to a specific professional; they may know their insurance coverage copay or not worry about it until after. What if the parent delayed getting X-rays because they thought the child was whining? If the parent did not see the severity, making the child wait several days to receive treatment- that parent might feel guilt for the pain the child is experiencing. The parent may feel embarrassed or defensive for delaying treatment. Or maybe the child was doing something crazy, like jumping off the top of the playground. The caregiver may retell this story with a supportive tone or a shaming, "how stupid" voice. Or the parent was playing tag with the child in the yard, and the child tripped and hurt her ankle that way - the parent did not directly harm but was involved in the cause. What if the parent brings in the child and gives the therapist a list of ways they have supported and tried to identify the sprained ankle? Some practitioners may say you overstepped. What if the parent brought in the child and did not put ice on the ankle or elevate it? Some practitioners may say, "You did not do enough." What if, while waiting for treatment, the gym teacher keeps calling to inform the child will have a failing grade due to their lack of participation? Will the parent be mad at the teacher, the child, or themself?

Many parents/caregivers share similar experiences and emotions with placing their children in therapy. Fears for their child, fears of how professionals will view them, the grief of circumstances, uncertainty in hiring a therapist, vulnerability hangovers, and practical issues like babysitters, payment, and scheduling. Most families have a similar path in pursuing help. First, a deficit or gap between parental/societal expectations and child performance is recognized. "Deficit" is not necessarily negative. It is just a gap between expectation and performance: I want to enhance my child's ability to communicate, or we need additional strategies to support my child's stress. Sometimes the deficit is phrased negatively: This child is making our family miserable, or we can't handle their tantrums and no one wants to be around them. Secondly, the parent/caregiver uses the tools within their tool- box- these may be safe and supportive or maladaptive and dangerous tools. Acknowledging the deficit and avoiding it is also a strategy within a toolbox. Non-action is a self-preservation tool, especially with parents directly contributing to dangerous environments. Often, the child will not "improve" or improve at the rate the caregiver expects. Thirdly, there may be a significant catalyst moment (suspension from school, self-harm attempt), or they realize the need for external help outweighs their ability to resolve as a family unit. Then help is sought for the person perceived to need it, not always the person who truly needs it. Parents/caregivers often seek therapy when there is a gap between parental expectations and child performance. It is less likely for parents/caregivers to seek therapy to better their parenting. The efficacy of treatment depends on the mode of treatment, the therapist's qualifications and training, client buy-in, and their support system.

Treatment efficacy depends on the appropriate mode of treatment and the therapist's qualifications and training. I encourage therapy and treatment; I encourage meds as they can be life-saving. I also encourage research of the appropriate services. Overwhelmed caregivers may seek "triage" care for our children - "What medicine will stop this behavior? What is the emergency response? How do we minimize the damage?" Chapter 4 will address emergencies and how to set up a support system. Ongoing, stabilizing treatment is important for a family unit to thrive. The right mode of treatment is essential for long-term success. Play therapy, Art therapy, and Somatic therapies can help tap into some of these "non-verbal" neural experiences. Additionally, if you or your child experienced early years trauma- an occupational therapist can give insight into what reflexes did not develop properly within the body. EMDR and Brainspotting are other approaches to tap into unprocessed memories.

Neural Affective Relational Model (NARM) is a therapeutic approach focused on individuals with C-PTSD. It incorporates a bottom-up and top-down approach to connect with the body. Internal Family Systems (IFS) is an approach appropriate for children and adults. As a caregiver- you have the right to ask questions of the therapist in an initial interview. Therapists and social workers pursue further education beyond their college degrees. Trauma, dissociation, and transracial adoptions are additional areas of expertise for therapists and social workers. Not all therapists have training in these areas. It would be best to ask about their trauma and dissociation qualifications. Ask if they are content or process focused. Ask if there are specific diagnoses they find challenging and those they prefer to work with. Ask about their understanding of neurodivergence. These questions help decide if a therapist is a right fit.

CBT and DBT can be effective in some situations, are research-based, and most insurance companies recommend them. From a "trauma stored in the body" approach, these are not effective without a trauma and somatic lens. Additionally, for individuals who do not have a basis of self-trust, trying to believe certain thoughts without that reality existing within your body feels like gaslighting. Remember - neurodivergent brains will process these forms of therapy differently than a neurotypical brain. If you have done therapy and it does not work, you are allowed to leave and find a better fit. We have experienced excellent therapists who were supremely helpful. We have experienced amazing therapists who did not have the toolbox we needed. Behavior training will not work with a child/adult who experiences dissociation states or ongoing dissociation. The ANP may comply with behavioral changes. EPs or dissociative shifts will be wary of processes they did not give consent to, which may threaten their communication. An uninformed therapist will not have the tools necessary to navigate these shifts.

Healing stalls when memories collide with lived experiences. Have you ever had a different memory than a sibling or parent? These different memories sometimes indicate a different perspective (what I remember as a child vs. what the adult remembered). Sometimes though, it may be a reflection of dissociation and experiences of different internal parts. I worked with one individual who experienced continual ongoing distress even though they had years of therapy and medications. They had "done the work". They continued to experience impressions/memories of intense violence and rape occurring at a young age. These memories could never identify a perpetrator or what had actually happened. These memories remained separate from what they knew about their lived experiences and information shared by adults. However, the sensation and memories were real and palpable to this individual. At the time, I did spiritual counseling focused on internal healing. In a session, she was processing her confusion and ongoing distress. Following her process, I would ask questions that prompted self-guidance and safety by sifting her internal states. Listening to her inner self process reminded us of manic episodes in her early adult years. Her inner child-self had experienced those through her, including various sexual experiences. Experiencing normative sexual experiences, not to mention additional incidents of assault and violence, were understandably overwhelming and violating to this younger self-state. Our goal was to bring relief to her inner child, who felt violated and in pain. "I believe you" is a powerful truth our inner parts need to hear. We can not trust our selves if we do not truly trust our self. As we processed these memories, the "older self" explained to the "younger self" about some of these experiences. They explained their current relationship to develop predictable expectations for the younger self. They apologized for their pain and offered ways of comfort and connection. The individual experienced a reduction in the flood of memories and bombardment of perceptions. The goal is not to decide what "actually happened", but to build a bridge of trust between a disconnected self. Many people externally live in a way that appears "thriving" or "society approved", yet inside have debilitating thoughts of failure, disconnect, and haunted memories. Without a suitable therapy mode or a therapist with the fitting tools, they may feel "incurable". This "incurable" feeling often echoes the voices of isolated EPs.

Client motivation and their support system directly impact treatment efficacy. By effective, I mean developing self-acceptance, ongoing developmental growth, and decreasing dangerous/maladaptive behaviors over time. If the caregiver has participated in therapy for themself, has reflected and adapted their parenting approaches, and places their child in therapy, the therapeutic process is more likely to be effective. This may mean the child has more outbursts to "test out" the safe space. It may look like the child expresses themself and reminds the parent to reciprocate respect. It will not look like a "perfect" child- because that is not developmentally appropriate. Healing will not mean the removal of all memories or pain but will provide a safe framework for the ongoing processing of previous life experiences. If the family unit is the child's home of origin, the therapeutic process will involve parents/caregivers working with the child to maintain a safe and connected space. It requires buy-in from all parties. The therapist can create a safety plan and encourage repair strategies to prevent relapses of behavior (from parents or children). If the caregiver has cultivated an environment of danger and placed their child within therapy, there will be stunted growth. A child living in a "turned off" dissociated state with caregivers using dissociative strategies will be unable to maintain long-term behavioral improvements. Their brain needs to conserve energy for survival.

My spouse and I desperately needed the stress and chaos to end. We had a deficit in expectations and performance. We had used all the tools in our toolbox, acquired more, and were still stuck. As time drags on - dissociative strategies are normalized, and families can lose sight of what is possible within their family. A year before we learned about dissociation and self-states, we had a strenuous series of days dealing with these odd, dangerous behaviors with one child. I started to pray, "Whatever is bad in him needs to be removed." To some who are not of a particular religious affiliation, this may understandably feel absurd, but for those of us who grew up understanding that any "off behavior or heart issue" can be healed by God, it felt reasonable. Unfortunately, many traumatized individuals are labeled as possessed, having dark hearts, or being evil. These labels attribute the internal turmoil as an individual issue without recognizing the responsibility of a family system and community. We questioned our belief system as my husband and I wrestled with the emotional, spiritual, mental, and physical realities of a child not being "freed" from their internal turmoil. [Side Note: as parents, we often seek medications for our kids and have them do treatment that we are unwilling to do ourselves. We place the burden of family stress on them, instead of distributing the bulk of responsibility to the parents.]

In this particular moment, the stress, overwhelm, grief, and uncertainty led me to declare "darkness out of him." I felt an internal prompt. Some may describe it as an internal knowing, but to me, I recognize it as a voice of Love. It said, "You do not have authority to send anything out of him, no part of him is bad." This challenged our views of an internally haunted child with a theological lens that teaches evil is constantly attacking. We wrestled with these experiences until a year later when we began this journey to discover his various self-states and their role in his life. We realized our own unhealed internal lives as adults had a role to play in cultivating a safer environment. My spouse and I had zero authority to dismiss these dark parts of him because these were all valid, good, amazing parts of him. They just needed a way to communicate and be valued. They needed a different way to express themselves and to feel connected. Rejecting or severing a part of one's self is what leads to self-hatred and harmful behaviors. This is why connection is always better than rejection. When we overlook dissociation and the need for embodiment, we risk severing off entire portions of people's existence and overlooking their inner story. When we overlook the parental/caregiver impact, there is a risk of placing all the family stress on the small shoulders of a child. That leads us to the impact of dissociation on intergenerational trauma.

-Intergenerational Trauma-

We have looked at the impact of dissociation on neural development and treatment efficacy. Now, let us look at the impact of dissociation on intergenerational trauma. A parent/caregiver raised with dissociative strategies will either continue using those strategies on their own children or decide to change. Maybe a parent experienced being spanked as a child and decides, "I turned out ok," and continues that pattern with their child. Or a parent says, "I am ok, but I want to communicate that hurting a loved one is not love," and they find other strategies to discipline and redirect. The parent choosing to change may receive support from their parents- "I am so glad that you found a different way to treat your kids. I was so overwhelmed and didn't know what to do!" Or their parents may view the shift as a threat or judgment, "Well, it was ok that we spanked you because you were out of control. You aren't any better than us. Just wait until your kid makes you really angry." Intergenerational trauma is when the pain of one generation passes down to the next and often the next. Intergenerational healing requires one person to change. One person! If that person has family support, it will cause a rapid ripple in the intergenerational pattern. If the person's family ostracizes them for doing it differently, the ripples will be slower but just as important.

If these examples of trauma and dissociation are triggering, please skip to the next section. I try to avoid being graphic, but it is important to specifically address topics that we tend to avoid- so be kind to yourself and go at your own pace. Understanding the intergenerational impact does not excuse or recuse someone from their responsibility for causing harm. **The normalization of an event does not detract from it being trauma.** It does not matter that many adults within a generation lacked parenting skills and whooped their kids - it is still trauma. Though both vastly damage the victim, there is a psychological difference in the perpetrator between abuse and torture - abuse is irrational, torture is intentional. Both are wrong. Choosing to accurately label abhorrent events is powerful. Physical abuse is correlated with a loss of control and eruptive anger- like a volcano erupting. Sexual, medical, emotional abuse, and neglect can all be additional forms of abuse. Torture intends to establish control and dominance - think of a volcano constantly leaking lava. This can include forms of abuse, depriving food, neglecting daily hygiene, not allowing sleep, isolation, and extensive periods of discipline (wall squats for 45 minutes, kneeling on rice, etc). Intergenerational traumas are challenging to trace because families hold secrets that may make them look bad or memories they cannot reconcile. Sometimes people do not have a memory of what occurred. And sometimes, the pain inflicted was to prevent greater pain from occurring. It is sacred to acknowledge what happened, why, and give space for that awfulness to exist. When we acknowledge, we begin to embody freedom - freedom from family rules, societal burdens, and physical confinements. The following are some examples of intergenerational traumas.

One way intergenerational traumas are recognized is through a "felt sense" rather than a "known" fact. Families may pass down stories or warnings about individuals or behaviors in a vague way. For example, one family may strongly caution their daughters about sexual interactions, be suspicious of males, and give suggestions for self-defense and protection. This advice was not shared alongside healthy sexual advice, just warnings. Later in life, the parent shares a vague memory with her daughters about being sexually abused when younger. The parent does not have a clear memory but a somatic knowing and a "locked puzzle piece" memory. The daughters grew up terrified of sexual encounters but can now understand why the parent advised how they did, given the history. The daughters now have to decide whether to perpetuate the family advice to their children or process a healthy sexual ethic to pass on in their family.

Intergenerational traumas can also show up years later. An example is a house bustling early in the morning before school. Kids are eating, arguing, getting dressed, and gathering belongings. Someone is being challenging, and the mom screams to silence the chaos. Next thing she knew, a gallon of milk exploded on the room's other side. She stared in shock, she threw it but had no idea that she threw it. Everyone looks at her like she is crazy, and she feels crazy. She then has to clean up the mess, help the kids get off to school, and does not have time to see if they are ok. The kids go to school, some feel disconnected for the day, and others laugh off what happened. If this happens frequently, the kids may connect early mornings with a time to be "shut down" to avoid triggering the parent. Sometimes we do not know the impact until years later- and one kid is now an adult living with their partner. It is in the morning before work, and the partner reaches into the fridge to grab a gallon of milk. The adult flashes back to that morning as a child and shutdowns, feeling unsafe. Or maybe they yell, "Don't throw it". The partner looks at them in shock at the abnormal response.

Intergenerational traumas can be debilitating. A mom stuck in the mental state of a 14-year-old, due to the ongoing sexual abuse from her father, being shamed and manipulated, and never receiving help - she maintains a fairly childlike demeanor. She gets married and has kids- but cannot take care of her house and children. As she gets older, her brain has been carrying the dual state of her existence for a very long time. The brain gets tired more quickly, and she is unable to take care of herself. Previously viewed as quirky, these behaviors are reflections of an inner self still seeking support and compassion. Her children grow up with a mom present in the body but not always in her mind.

Problematic systems can cause intergenerational traumas. Obviously slavery caused harm to generations of people. The Enslaved experienced wounds of displacement, beatings, dehumanization, rape, stolen children, and more. The enslavers experienced the echo of violence - when we are violent and dehumanizing to others, it cuts away at our own souls and establishes a lineage of violence. Refugees who escape atrocities just to be met with rejection at their place of refuge. Families split apart by war and genocide. Families torn through foster care and adoption. The pain and grief of these events is so vast, some will experience dissociation. To bring a child into a new home and say, "This is your new, forever home!" requires some element of disconnect within oneself. Potential disconnect from a former family, an identity, previous memories, and acceptance resistance. The strategies used to survive atrocities may be ineffective in younger generations living in different environments with different triggers.

Intergenerational traumas perpetuate a hierarchy. The "most powerful" prey on the most vulnerable member. We could assume the perpetrator themself had been preyed upon, which is why they chose this method to ascertain "safety via hierarchy". An often unspoken yet frequent occurrence within the US is the sexual abuse of young boys. Culturally, there is an assumption that female abuse is abuse. Overlooked male abuse is due to concepts of "toughness" and "not being a real man". These flawed beliefs lead to a disconnect with their inner younger self feeling betrayed by this domination. There is also shame in the cultural denial of their pain. A typical pattern within this grouping is that as these men age, they experience breakdowns within their key relationships, coinciding with raging anger and substance abuse. The inner child-self attempts to reconcile its past while the current self attempts to cover up to avoid the simmering pain. These men often experience such a high sense of "felt unsafety" that they cause their spouses and children to walk on eggshells and cower to their volatility. It is not the role of the wife to be this man's safe space - to be his inner child's rescuer from the pain experienced. Often these men will revere and hate their spouses- viewing them from a dissociative lens that causes an inconsistent relationship. Therapy, AA, and other supports do not work - because the inner child has not connected safely with the "oldest age" of the individual. They are not a safe host environment.

Intergenerational traumas develop a new trajectory when an individual chooses embodied practices and awareness - the brave choice to say "I will relearn how to feel and experience the world. I will treat my children and my children's children differently. I will interact with the world around me differently. I will respond to the pain from my parents differently than the family rules require." This shift is often incremental, bite-sized actionable steps with layers of emotion and somatic release occurring. A caregiver who chooses to shift the trajectory of intergenerational traumas sets the pace for their own relatives - "See! We can embody who we are intended to be! Life, joy, and brilliance, not walking on eggshells, forgetting memories, unsure of where we belong!"

When we ignore embodiment, we encourage dissociation. Dissociation encourages compliance; compliance is often the end goal of religious, educational, and governmental systems. Individuals who have learned to silence their discomfort expect others to remain silent in their own discomfort. And what we silence can eat away at our minds and bodies. Long after their ancestor has died, their fingerprints can remain. Individuals seething with hatred allow their inner selves to appease those who hurt them. When we acknowledge and respond to dissociation, the entire child gets to experience love on their developmental journey. They can receive the appropriate form of therapy and have a support system that encourages, not impedes, their thriving! What would it look like for families to be proud of their heritage AND work to improve it? What would happen if we did not look the other way when parents are overwhelmed but instead offered support? What would happen if we created communal grieving spaces that didn't rush people past their grief but let them feel, find roots and then find a new normal? What if we were more concerned about experiencing life and respecting a shared humanity than silencing our wounds? What if we cared about our own wounds more than micromanaging others? What if we believed, "I am worthy of wholeness!"?

5

Acceptance of the Entire Child

Let's take 10-15 minutes to chart a beginning point. "Your Family Map" will be a starting point for recognizing the relationship dynamics within your family. This activity can be done alone, or you could have your whole family make their own map!

Grab a piece of paper and write or draw each family member. They can be symbols, stick figures, or animals, whichever you prefer. Take some time and draw bridges, walls, rivers, trees, and mountains around/ near your family members. There is no right or wrong way; you can be as detailed or basic as you prefer. After you have drawn, look at your map.

Are some people connected with roads and bridges and others isolated? Are some people surrounded by trees and others rocks? Did you draw some people or landmarks larger and some smaller? Where did you place yourself? Where did you place the family member you have the most challenging time with? Where did you place the family member you feel closest with?

As you look at the map and ask some of these questions - let yourself relax, shoulders drop from your ears. Take several deep breaths. You are where you are - there is no right or wrong about your placement on the map. It just is. As lands shift over time, you and your family can also shift! Keep this map as a reference point to check growth six months from now.

The structure of a family unit sets the pace for the structure of a child's internal life. A fractured child often indicates a fractured family structure. These patterns are passed down from generation to generation. It is a bold, brave choice to address the adult rifts contributing to a family's disruption. This is an act of love to address any disconnects within oneself instead of placing those burdens on a child. You deserved to experience the joy and safety of being accepted in your entire existence as a child. Your mistakes embraced as growing pains and not sins. Your hobbies seen as art and not clutter. Your questions heard as curiosities and not nagging. Your skinned knees an invitation to comfort and not chastise. Your rebellion accepted as growing wings and not shame on your family. Encouraged to feel, know, think, experience, and breathe freely. And if heartbreakingly that was not the case - you can cultivate that for yourself and your own children.

Curiosity allows us to enter into the sacred space of another. If you have a child who stems - tapping a pencil, tiptoeing around a room, spinning in a circle, humming- curiously join in. Learn what they experience. Curiously, join in if your child is constantly ripping pencil parts, chewing on clothes, or tearing holes in their sweater. How much effort does that take? How much pressure are they using? What could be impacting that? If your child resists certain meals - curiously experiment with them - are burritos too squishy and need a crunch? What does it harm to have an "upside down" eating day? When you give an instruction, and your child collapses instead of complies, "I bet you had a lot of other instructions at school today; how many times were you told what to do today? That must be exhausting!" Curiosity leads to connection.

Creating a safe space to feel and exist allows compassion to flow. When caregivers are tense, we struggle to create a safe space. Rigid spaces birth rigid responses. Safe spaces birth safe responses. Compassion can include high accountability but will not shame or force disconnection.

Creating a safe space means the caregivers have realized there is a boundary to their feelings, and they experience their own embodied feelings. Then they can give their children a contained space for the overflow of emotions. Whether it is a child collapsed from the anxiety of existential thoughts or a child chased by haunted memories, or a child unable to escape thoughts of suicidal ideation - caregivers can provide a safe space to hold these vast treasures from our children. No thought is too big. No thought will divide our connection. You are not dangerous or unwanted. You are not too scary or too unsteady for those who love you. Compassion is not about the feeling oozing off the caregiver but the safe space created for the recipient. Compassion steadies connection.

These lead to cultivating an intentional response. Emergencies are not always emergencies, and feeling frantic is often an internal response to a previous situation. Steady connection can help us make calm choices with a long-term vision. A curious caregiver will consider if the child feels safe and if this is a "now" issue or a developmental stage to weave into the child's growth. A compassionate caregiver will realize that rage may be aimed at them even if it is not their fault. A connected caregiver will create space for all the facets of a child without shaming them. This environment will allow a child to develop all the parts of their inner life at a natural pace.

Creating a safe space for children who have experienced traumas and dissociation requires serious work on the caregiver's part. We have not "saved" a child to remove them from one type of neglect and insert them into another kind of neglect. **A child is the sum of all of their parts**. Each part needs to be valued and respected. This requires extensive self-work on the part of the parent. Every person in the family benefits from adjusting to creating a safe, shame-free space. The greatest gift we can give our children is to provide a safe space to exist freely within their current existence. The child can experience love and accountability, be heard and affirmed, and be treasured and challenged. If you have been frustrated and exhausted - I hope this book brings you hope. Sometimes we don't realize that the battle trenches we dug are now our tombs.

What we thought was our protection can end up being our end. We can dig out, climb out of the trenches, and let our inner self and our kids know that there is no war with them. It is not weak, but it is tenderly vulnerable. There is new territory to explore together if we can curiously and compassionately embrace all the parts of our children and our selves.

This book began with theories and definitions. The same information within those chapters took my spouse and me several years to unlearn old ways and learn new concepts. Then it was longer to integrate these concepts and applications in a way that flowed naturally. Growth is a spiral (picture a slinky), not linear (picture a ruler). As you learn, you will face situations that your neural pathways approach in a specific way. Remember, your neural pathway are a well-traveled path! Shifting your behavior and response will require traveling on a new pathway-this may feel awkward, challenging, and ineffective. The more we travel a pathway, the less resistance our brain releases. There is no award for the quickest learning curve - we each are on unique paths. As the book focuses on the practical, you can return to earlier chapters to reinforce your practice or pick one skill to work on. The book's next section begins with eight questions to guide your approach to parenting a child with dissociation. Then using the 4 C's lens (curiosity, compassion, connection, and cultivation), I share some of our experiences and learnings for parents and siblings connected to dissociation.

6

Questions to Guide Connective Strategies

The following 8 questions will help replace dissociative strategies with connective strategies. A child, much like a starfish, responds to their environment. The ability to regrow and repair ruptured parts is impacted by a hostile or safe habitat. I recommend that you pick one question to focus on for practical application. Spend at least a week to 6 months checking in with yourself during interactions with your kids. When you feel semi-confident with that one, pick another question to focus on.

Am I (the adult) regulated?
Do they feel safe?
Is this an emergency?
What is the goal?
Does this help the child connect to themselves?
Does the child consent to this?
What age/skill am I addressing?
Does this build capacity?

1. Am I, the adult, regulated?

The responsibility lies on the adult to regulate their own emotions and responses. This concept is unpacked more in the following chapter on Parenting. Self-regulation does not mean you will love what has happened or have a perfect idea of how to resolve a situation. Self-regulation means you will identify and respond to your emotions and actions. You will recognize if you need to press pause on the interaction or need to get backup support. You will recognize if there is an inner part of you that needs to feel safe before being a safe person for your child. Reparenting yourself alongside your child is challenging and brave. Remember - self-regulation is recognizing your response and your nervous system state and responding to yourself first.

2. Do they feel safe?

This question can begin with reflections by the caregiver, "Am I creating a safe environment?" But then it must expand to "Does the child feel safe?" And "Do all the parts of the child feel safe?" The adult may assume an environment is "safe," but the child's past or present experience tells them otherwise. Having the curiosity to enter into their experience is essential for perspective. A safe environment is going to be safe physically and emotionally. Some aspects of physical safety may depend on your child or your situation. For example, when our children first moved in, their experience of neglect told them that new homes might not have food. We had the menu listed on the fridge but chose to put cereal canisters on the counter so there would be a constant visual of food. A child who is hyper-vigilant from experiences of violence may need specific objects placed out of view (kitchen knives being an example) or need a warning before you high-five. Another child may need to walk around the house and help you lock doors at night. These "safety procedures" are used to establish a felt sense of safety. Over time, the need for these procedures may diminish and, in our experience, only return in times of emotional stress. A safe environment will have high predictability- routine listed, chances to give feedback on activities, help packing snacks for a trip, and discussion of expectations. Some children need a reminder every few hours; others can handle a week's breakdown. As capacity builds, there can be more flexibility and even capacity for unexpected plans.

My husband and I were sometimes "loud" responders. At times it would startle the kids if our voices were not predictable. I had to choose to adjust how I'd respond if it were in a silly but startling way- their felt-safety was more important than me holding on to my tone. Comfort foods or comfort items are important during transitions. A "safe" person on-site at school or clubs is essential. One of my children needed to have my number memorized but never called me; other children did not want to memorize my phone number but knew they could email me from school. Safety may include giving space to odd behaviors- some kids will sleep on the floor until they feel secure to move to their bed, others will want to wear clothes that are too small because of memories, tell imaginative stories, insist on only a certain meal repeatedly, etc. Allowing the child to determine the pace of their acceptance of an environment is important. Self-pacing was vital for my children coming from a foster care environment into a permanent home environment. If a child does experience dissociation in mild to more intense states-predictability, visual cues, and apparent safety are very important.

A meaningful way to establish trust is to ask your child, "What helps you feel safe, and what makes you feel unsafe in this house?" Share with them a time or situation when you felt unsafe when you were younger. Giving children control over their environment can empower children with Anxiety and PTSD. This is also true of ASD children, ADHD, and other diagnoses- their ability to contribute to their environment will impact their felt level of safety. A child who expresses discomfort with textures, tastes, and pace of schedule will have a dysregulated nervous system if they cannot communicate a need connected to the sensory input. If they communicate or adapt, their nervous system may stay within the zone of functioning. For example, after a loud, stressful day at school, one child sat down to dinner and started to yell because of the chewing sounds. They walked away and returned with headphones.

They were feeling an onslaught of sensory experiences but adapted and returned to dinner. When this specific child was younger, they could not communicate or adapt. As parents, we did not have the tools to help- the child's dysregulation led to an ongoing felt sense of "unsafety" within their body.

3. What is an emergency?

A family unit under constant stress will see every situation as an emergency or overlook serious red flags. Anxiety causes the brain to jumble our signals - adrenaline may rush at the wrong time, and we overreact. Over-reacting causes exhaustion and depletion of energy. Then when something serious is occurring, you may numb out or over-look it. A parent raised in a home with high-stress parents may learn to dissociate during stressful situations. Their "big behaviors" are viewed as intentional inconveniences. Additionally, if someone is hyper-vigilant about these stressors, they may misread the small cues and overreact. I would sense my child being frantic and begin feeling frantic, anticipating a meltdown. Then I would react from the "managing a meltdown" point instead of the pre-meltdown stage they were experiencing. As we become attuned to our responses and triggers, we better assess what an emergency is and what is baseline child behavior.

Here are a few sample scenarios to think through:
-A child is distraught that they did not get to do an activity. They are crying and screaming. Their emotional response is intense, but nothing needs to be resolved. After attempting time together to help them regulate, they are now in their room alone. No one is in danger, and any items the child can break (blanket, dresser) are replaceable. Does this feel like an emergency? Do you have a plan for the stress the sounds bring to the other children? Does one partner feel the child's stress more than another? Do you have a way to check-in on the child? Do you have a plan to reconnect when they calm down?

-A child is over-stimulated after a long day at school. It is bed-time and they are unable to settle. Other children are in bed, and both parents are tired. The child starts throwing things at the other child with whom they share a room. How do you respond? Do you remove the other child into a calmer space so they aren't bothered? Do you get the instigating child to leave the room? What if they refuse? What if the 10-year-old is like a 2-year-old at bedtime until they stabilize their self-state? Would that impact your response? After an intense night, how do you regroup the next day?

-A child has been teasing their sibling. After an extensive time, the aggravated sibling starts trying to attack the instigator. How do you respond? Do you feel yourself siding with one of them over the other? Do the size of your children impact how you view their behavior (toddlers vs. teens)? Do you have a backup person you can call for help? Who do the children aim their anger at when the fight ends? Who else is impacted by this situation? How do you resolve it?

-A child has been unable to follow directions all day. The parent needs a break and has the child be in their room to "rest". The parent is outside and looks up to see the child's window open and them pushing out their window screen from the second story. What do you do? What do you feel? What do you imagine is going through the kid's mind? What if the child is so stressed they can't think of anything else to do? If they are "getting attention," what are they getting attention for?

-A child has been overstimulated all day. By dinner, they are agitated and do not like the food in front of them. They start pacing the house, muttering under their breath constantly. Any attempt to engage leads to a further escalation of emotions. The child walks out the front door. It has been 25 minutes, and the child is not home yet. What do you do? What do you feel? What do you imagine is going through the kid's mind? Is your neighborhood safe enough for them to wander and return or are there safety concerns? What are the "worst case" scenarios going through your mind? Can you pause them to figure out a plan? Do you have a spouse or neighbor you can trust to divide up and scan the neighborhood? What would require a call to emergency services - length of time gone, area of the neighborhood, weather/appropriate clothing?

-You walk into a room and see an older sibling inappropriately touching a younger sibling's private parts. The older sibling immediately gets defensive and says it was an accident, and the younger sibling does not have much of a response. What do you do? What do you feel? What emotions rush over you? What is your own lived experience with this? Who do you contact for help? What worst-case scenarios are running through your head? How do you help without causing further harm? How do you get support for both children? What are the safety precautions you must now use in the house? What will your response be to people who push back on your safety precautions but do not need to know details?

-It is dinner time, and one of your children is not at the table. You holler for them, and they do not show up. You assume that the child is hiding or out playing with friends. After a while, you search the house and find your child duct-taped to the punching bag in the basement. Their older sibling and friend taped them and left them in the dark. What do you do? What feelings do you experience? What is your child experiencing? What excuses come to mind? What boundaries were crossed? What is an appropriate consequence or teaching for the older child? How do you ensure the younger child feels safe?

Determining what is and isn't an emergency boils down to **1.** "Is someone's life in danger?" **2.** "Is someone being treated dangerously and/or without consent (to their body, mind)?" Differentiate between an emergency triage and a serious long-term plan with your partner or support system. When our nervous system floods with adrenaline- our minds and bodies are in protection and survival mode. My nervous system floods when I discover a new behavior or a serious situation. My system reads this flood of adrenaline and cortisol as "Danger"! Imagine red flashing lights and sirens resounding in my head, and often the child is sitting there doing a behavior they have done dozens of times before

- without anyone knowing. My elevated response signaling "danger" confuses a child whose behavior was probably calming to their nervous system. It is crucial for me to step back and determine what is "dangerous" (requiring immediate help), what is "serious" and needs a long-term plan, or what is a new behavior I need to wrap my brain around.

Developing a plan allows the caregiver to not jump to survival mode as quickly. When we already live in survival mode, it requires bite-size chunks of modification over-time. Additionally, depending on the age of the children - their involvement in the plan provides them with buy-in and supporting themself. We have one child who likes to take long walks when upset - however, we had to place boundaries around walking in the dark and the areas they walk. Establishing which items are needed for sensory stimulation to punch or pull or receive pressure is helpful. If I make space for those feelings to flow safely and supported, the child can expand their capacity to experience emotions. Sometimes having those feelings flow in a safe and supported way will mean having the support of a therapist, a safe family member, or medication. When our children see us respond to their instability with the fear of their dangers, they internalize the message, "I am dangerous. I cause harm. People are scared of me." Those kids learn to stay safe in that space of exhibiting dangerous and harmful behaviors. Instead, we can demonstrate, "This is scary for all of us - you included!" while creating a safe space to hold their terrifying feelings tenderly.

Harm reduction takes a damaging behavior and works to reduce it over time safely. Behavior is communication. We may temporarily ignore behavior that does not cause serious harm, focusing on building the child's capacity and slowly exchanging coping mechanisms. For example, a child bumping their head on a wall - the bumping is a sensory input expressing distress or stimulation. If it is not damaging them and you can handle the sound, you can let the behavior continue. You can look for the underlying cause and attempt replacement behaviors. Some forms of self-harm are an attempt to escape the person's sensory input or mental input. When we make someone stop that behavior, they do not have a way to "escape" themself except dissociate. Getting curious about what they are experiencing is vital for meeting them in that place of suffering and helping them to feel safe. If you redirect, "Don't scratch your skin, you'll get sores!" but their skin literally feels like it is "crawling with bugs," - it is not addressing the actual need. Providing medicine or lotion may help in the interim, but the mind will jump to a different way to release its stress unless we compassionately address the root cause. An individual exhibiting self-harm behaviors will often carry a layer of fear of isolation - especially if there has not been a history of open conversation and support. If we belittle the expressions of discomfort and pain our children have in minor areas, they have no reason to trust we will take them seriously in a significant issue. Additionally, if the child has never acquired self-regulation skills, we are shaming them for not using a skill they never learned.

Develop a scale to communicate the level of assistance needed for true emergencies. The caregiver can share this with their support system. It may look like this: 1- the kids are on edge, and I need some time alone this evening. 3 - the kids are ok, but I am at my wits end and may explode. 5- emergency, I cannot handle this stress and need reinforcements. For a child, it will depend on their stress response. Suppose you have a child who has violent behaviors and is unable to regulate themself. In that case, another child may need to state, "It's a level 5 emergency" vs. "It's a level 3, waiting for explosion". Equipping our kids to put themselves in a secure place is important. As the child with volatile behaviors grows, it is a goal for them to learn to recognize their internal experience and then ask for or use regulating strategies before it explodes. Some children will spiral before dissociating to a "secure" mental state. Others will experience an "on-off" switch. The child in the spiral will begin to feel the momentum pick up and feed off the cues of those external to them. As they feel out of control, they see and sense people around them being scared of them, they feel scared of themself, their internal state becomes even more dysregulated, and their level goes from a 3 to a 4 or a 5. By removing external stimulus that does not contribute to stability, we can help the child not to experience additional distress.

For a child who expresses "escapism" through suicidal ideation, it is important in a low-stress time to come up with a scale so they can ask for help. Their baseline of 1, may be different from yours. Their "1" may still include a high level of physical or mental discomfort; they may not have a "1" that is all calm. One child kept saying, "I need to get out of this. I can't handle this anymore. This is too much for me, I just want to die." And in discussions with their therapist, we collectively agreed this meant, "I am feeling overwhelmed so intensely I need to escape this current moment or my body drastically". Our emotions and fears as parents can add a layer of intensity to our kids, making it harder for them to deal with their current existence. When I could step back and say, "He is at level 3. He needs soothing foods, space from sounds, super soft clothes, and space from other humans in the house," it would give the child space to regulate. He didn't have to worry about managing himself and the adults in the house. Finding a therapist and medication is important for the child and family to receive ongoing help. If the lived experience of a child is so intense, they will resist embodiment. Dissociation decreases for a child given support to gauge their own experience. Their connection to self will increase, resulting in greater self-awareness, self-support, and hopefully self-love.

4. What is the goal?

Identifying the goal will guide the interaction between adults and children. Triage, maintenance, and long-term are different categories of goals. A triage goal will address an immediate dangerous behavior. Maintenance goals focus on capacity building. Long-term goals focus on future independence. Using a basic example of crossing the road: the triage goal is to stop a child from running across the street as a car is approaching (we may yell, grab the child, etc.), maintenance goal is to practice together during play time (practice looking both ways, play red light green light at the street), and the long-term goal is for the child to look both ways and cross the street to the mailbox. As the parent, you take into account the development and capability of your individual child. Another goal may be to encourage the development of a child's regressed self-states. For example, if a child is sucking their thumb and I am concerned about teeth - I also need to balance if they need soothing missed from early years. My response to removing a comfort item or comfort response will depend on the level of safety this child feels.

As I was learning these concepts and putting them into practice, I aimed to focus on my responses and not on my children's actions. I would not address the situation if I could not trust my response as curious and compassionate. It was important to me to create a safe internal space for myself and, by extension, my children. Having a goal is like having an anchor. Instead of getting swept up in chaos or emotions from family, I could say, "I am focusing on this one thing." It anchored me to the developmental skill of a child or myself. This intentional "slowing down" also sends a signal to the brain - "Hey, I gotchu. We are not frantic. We have a plan." This allows the body to shift from our stress responses to calm and processing responses. Explaining my goal to the child (and their ANP) clarified our interactions. They knew the goal might shift in a few months, that the parent was taking care of themself first, and that the ANP was responsible for baseline goals/expectations at the time. Clarity reduced the child's need to constantly "test" me and my responses. Stability brought felt-safety.

5. Does this help the child connect to themself?

A child raised with healthy attachment and connection to a parent will be attached to the parent and, as they age, will begin to shift those attachments. In a healthy environment, a child learns to co-regulate their emotions from a caregiver. The child will have a big feeling, and the parent will reflect and model the ability to handle the big emotion. Often, there are either rifts with attachment in a child's younger years and the child takes on the "adult role" in co-regulation. There is a higher likelihood of dissociative tendencies and dissociation-in-development for these children. To be a safe, compassionate guide, the child must connect with their inner fractured self. When someone has dissociated and has several ages internally - it is more important to feel safe with and connect with their stable self before connecting with a caregiver. Teaching a child to connect to themself is to trust themself.

Caregivers from the family of origin must recognize that there may be a dissociated portion of the child with its own memories and connections. Each of those will have a different path to repair with the parental unit. Additionally, you are allowed to want a relationship with your child, but they must have the space to connect with themself first. For example, if the child is 13 and has positive experiences with their mom but seems to shift in aggression, it could be a younger age that is upset at them for being open to a relationship with their mom. You do not want to encourage further distrust within them - so continue to provide a curious space and compassionate pace in the current age and other parts.

As an adoptive mom of older children, the kids had experienced rifts with other maternal figures before me. Even though I was "Mom", I knew that that title wasn't automatically assumed. As I changed my approach and created safe, secure spaces for every aspect of them to exist-different ages would "peek" out to test the waters. I realized that not every age knew what role I was for them - sometimes, that meant helping them re-explain their story, bringing out old pictures, and reminding them of good connections with their bio mom. As a parent, I have to assess my end game - is it a child attaching to me, must they embrace my version of "mom", or do I let the child exist in their safest form?

Statements of praise may cause recoil in a child not connected to themself. I would share with teachers, "Please only make observation statements to child X. If you praise or compliment, they will sabotage." To a child who has internal disconnections, external praise indicates a threat of dependance on another person. The positive emotion can signal a risk: there will be disappointment and rejection if I let them down. "Wow! You did a great job cleaning up your mess!" will incite the child (or their internal selves) to not clean up next time or potentially sabotage the positive. It can also cause turmoil between inner parts that are succeeding and those that are failing and feel rejected. "I see you put the blocks in their container and the pencils on the desk." A factual statement can be co-agreed upon by the child and their internal parts. Depending on the child, you could expand with, "What did you observe about cleaning up?" or "You contributed to this classroom as a safe space." or "Do you have a suggestion for cleaning up next time?" Overtime, I learned to recognize which of my children's fronting parts were present, by how they received or responded to praise. Encouraging self-connection is vital for their ongoing internal cohesion.

6. Does the child have consent to this process?

Consent is agreement or permission. Assent is expressing approval in sound or action. Taught from a young age, a child will learn they may express "yes" or "no" to situations. A child is not always allowed to consent to the choices in their life: having to wear shoes in a store, not playing with sharp glass, or being forced to take an antibiotic. Plenty of times, a child must comply with instructions they do not want to follow. Consent and assent are developed over time within healthy environments that also allow a child to disagree or opt. These areas of expected compliance will vary for each family based on family history, medical diagnoses, and a child's mental functioning. Children raised in an environment of trauma, unsafe spaces, and unsafe responses will have experienced a breach of their consent boundary. They may have learned that adults would ignore their "no", crossing their physical and mental boundaries. For a child who has experienced a breach of their "consent boundary", it is challenging to know if choices are because they want to or because the adult is coercing or manipulating them.

When I view a child prone to dissociation, I realize that their ANP may consent and their EP is resistant. It may look like the child is ambivalent or unable to decide on an activity. While the ANP attempts to enjoy a game with the family, the EP may be "internally resisting".

Resistance can appear as sensory discomfort, a foggy brain, and other internal disruptions until the child loses focus on the game. Outwardly it will look disruptive. The child may not have the vocabulary to describe what happened. The ANP, focusing on daily functions and survival, will be more likely to comply than assert a "no". Over time, they learn that compliance leads to not being harmed. The child does not develop an age-appropriate ability to say "no". Even though it appears they are willfully participating in family activities, they may have an internal resistance that feels coerced.

Returning to the discussion about neural framework - if your child is a "bottom-up" thinker, it may appear they are intentionally non-compliant and defiant. In reality, they need to understand the process that impacts the choice and poke holes in the traditional approach to see if it IS the best way. When bottom-up thinking layers with dissociation in age-selfs, it can appear to be a very defiant jumbled kiddo. Developing consent requires including children in problem-solving, establishing goals, and allowing them to mess up. Some children seem to collapse when given options or the chance to say "yes" or "no". This "collapse" indicates a small capacity for buy-in. They could have anxiety about the result of their choice, may feel fear or dread, or may not care. Developing consent requires safe practice spaces to choose wrongly- to say "yes" to the wrong thing and see that the world does not fall apart. Experimenting builds their capacity to say "yes" to big things and be prepared when a choice does not go as planned.

7. What is the age/developmental skill to address?

This foundational concept will impact what issues you choose to address and what you place on the back burner. For example, a child unable to participate in group work at school (a reasonable expectation of a 7th grader) may need tiered skills to focus on completing work individually and the ability to handle the transition of "leader" from teacher to peer presenter. If this child can barely handle "parallel play", from a developmental perspective, they cannot yet handle interactive play/

assignments. Picture a child who is assigned the chore of washing dishes but finds themself entranced with playing in the water. If their age is 14 and their developmental stage is 14, I expect them to complete the task and find another time to play in the water. If their age is 14 and their developmental stage is 5, then occasionally playing in the water while being redirected is expected.

Neurodivergent children develop asynchronously. They will often spiral heavily into one area of development, and another will "lack". Then their brain shift gears and pours energy into another skill. What we used to call "late bloomers" are actually successful energy users! If they mastered every skill at the "developmentally appropriate time", they would be void of all energy. One of my Autistic children was very "by the book" and had high anxiety about not meeting expectations of teachers and adults. When they were in 7th grade, they told me about taking the long way around the building from one class to the next. They felt independent and excited about marginally breaking a rule. They needed to practice rule-breaking (an important developmental stage) and thinking through how to handle if they got in trouble. When I see a child going nonverbal, I know energy is being redirected into another physical or mental process. If the child is struggling with a skill or interaction, I will need to reflect on what scaffolded skills may they have missed before this.

Balancing developmental and chronological age is sometimes tricky because consequences for an older child are not always age-appropriate for younger children. We often have to walk with feet in two worlds - the world of chronological age and the world of developmental age. If my child gets a school consequence for their behavior, it will match their chronological age. I work with the child to ensure that their inner self is adequately supported and receiving developmental help while supporting the older self with its "real world" consequences. Emphasizing their positive choices, the experience as a learning opportunity, and their safety in connection helps to orient the focus of a consequence.

8. Does this build capacity?

Building capacity recognizes a deficit and sees a path to bridging the gap between expectation and performance. For example, I read about a therapist who played chess with new clients (children). The first few times, the therapist would play easy and let the child win. The goal was to build confidence and rapport. Then the therapist would increase the challenge level and would win a game. Depending on the impact of disappointment, the therapist would increase or decrease the level of challenge. To determine "What is the capacity for this?", think of the behavior, task, or issue you must address. Write down every step for that thing. List the emotional, mental, physical choices and actions required. You can identify what skill you will work on, or your child can help identify where the breakdown occurs. If the consequence of a poor choice does not also address building capacity - the child will not grow in their ability to shift behaviors and internal felt-safety.

After my family had five kids, I was drowning in overwhelm with household chores. Well-intentioned friends suggested that I had the kids all help with chores. The few times I attempted this, some kids made it worse than before, others "forgot", and one child efficiently completed the task. I did not have the capacity to follow through in a teaching and compassionate way. I just needed a clean house. Some of my kids did not have the capacity to complete a task and feel good about themself. Some of my kids needed more capacity to complete all the parts of a task. These issues can feel incredibly intense and hopeless when experienced daily. When I eventually recognized it was a capacity issue, we focused on the steps of building capacity. Personally, I cannot do a chore chart, but I can place post-its of chores on the cabinet, and the children get to pick their chores. I cannot follow up with five children simultaneously, but I can give them 24 hours to complete it. For the children who stare at a room and don't know where to begin, I can provide a checklist of items to work on. When we back off from "frantic", it is easier to scaffold the growth necessary for a long-term goal.

Explore these 8 questions with curiosity. If a question stirs up anger, tension, or sadness - then pause. Give yourself compassionate space. If your partner or co-caregiver is agitated with these concepts - explore with curiosity. If it is not an "emergency" then we can explore, experiment and test what works best for our family and our children. Remember - if our nervous system is on edge it will take longer to absorb change. Connection and compassion with yourself will pave the way for cultivating rich environments of healing.

7

Parents and Caregivers

"Well meaning people keep saying to us, 'You did what any reasonable parents would have done.' But our child in his darkest hour needed us to be exceptional, not reasonable."
Todd Sturgeon, Father of Louisville shooter
Interview on April 27, 2023

If I were sitting across from you right now, I would want you to know this is a safe space. I would want you to know that it will get better, but it may look messier before it is better. I want you to know that all of this (pretend I am gesturing around with my hands) is not your fault. And I also want to gently say, as caregivers, you and I often contribute to the stress and pain in our houses. I want you to know that you are not alone, and yet I know how lonely it can feel not to have enough help or the right kind of ears to hear what help you need. I want you to know that what you feel is real, yet it is also a backlog of stress in our bodies. Your intuition is often right but is not always correct. I want you to know that you can try your best, and it still not be enough. And that is ok. I want you to know that every emergency is desperate, but every desperate thing is not an emergency. I want you to know that your hands are gentle, your voice is soft, and your heart is kind. I want you to know that your child is delightful, even if they are crazy- there is goodness in them. I want you to know that self-care only works if we feel safe. I want you to know we only feel safe once we slow down. I know you know it feels impossible to slow down when we feel chased. I know you can't stop being chased when you live with those who chase you, either within your mind or in your house. I want you to know that we cannot miraculously escape from the muck, but I can walk with you on the path that led my family and me out.

One day while the kids were at school, I thought, "Gosh, it's been really stressful. I'm gonna buy a bunch of Nerf guns and darts. When they come home from school, we can have a blast!" I was determined to lighten the mood in the house. All the kids came home, got snacks, and then I pulled out darts. Chaos ensued. Within 5 minutes, the house was under more stress than before. A few were still running and playing. One had hit the floor in a fetal position. Another was searching their face in the mirror for potential blood. What could have been, should have been, "fun" was experienced as dangerous. It felt unsafe to some. Other kids were pissed that the game ended early.

Reflection: How would you have felt in this situation as the parent? How would you have felt as a child? How would you have responded as the parent? How would your caregivers have responded to you when you were a child?

I spent some time feeling irritated. My initial response to irritation often leads me to look for someone to blame so that I can transfer the feeling of distress onto someone else. However, it was not the children's fault that I had spent money on Nerf guns and darts. It was not anyone's fault that they were shooting the Nerf guns as intended. It was not my fault for wanting to have "fun". And it wasn't the upset child's fault that they were scared and made the game end early. Not everyone has to love doing a Nerf gun battle. We could decide never to do that activity again, or we could choose to provide boundaries around it. As a family, we regrouped and devised rules for the game. People could opt out if they did not want to participate. We later encouraged those opting out to practice just shooting at the window - so they could get used to the sound of it and the "jump" in their hands. Months later, I saw one child staring at the others- she wanted to join in but still didn't feel safe. We made a rule that she could only be shot at by Dad, who would better handle respecting her space and helping her feel safe. Four years later, she will grab a Nerf gun and jump into battle with everyone else.

Parents and caregivers who aim for curiosity and compassion will be able to provide the connection needed for a foundation of safe relationships; then, they can cultivate long-term growth. Safety for the child assumes that you, as a parent, caregiver, grandparent, or teacher, will have that same curiosity and compassion for yourself and your own life experiences. We naturally respond from the toolbox of skills and strategies shown to us as children. Over time, we can inventory our toolbox, keep what works, and remove what does not. We will likely acquire new skills, strategies, and information over time. Expanding our tools is essential for parenting in a connected way. It is vital when parenting children of higher needs and/or diagnoses. Self-reflection and evaluation are imperative when parenting other people's children through adoption, family placements, or foster care. Parenting carries a tension between "opposites": grief and joy, curiosity and rigidity, expectations and acceptance. Each section in this chapter has reflective questions - I suggest you journal your responses, noticing what feels "doable" and what is daunting. Remember, we acquire new skills when we feel safe and connected!

Grief and Joy:

Grief and Joy are two sides of the same coin. These profound visceral experiences of life can feel daunting and drowning. Have you ever been upset about something and were advised, "Make a list of what you are thankful for?" Or "Well, at least you have _____ and should be happy!" Grief and Joy build capacity for each other. My feeble grasps at joy were fleeting as I tried to be "thankful" for our experiences. Think back to Chapter 2- from a top-down or neurotypical approach. "Declaring joy" is a starting point, then the brain pulls up evidence to support "joy", then our brain chooses an action path to align with this thought. A bottom-up approach begins with the sensory input- I am exhausted, I feel so stressed, kids are screaming, laundry is everywhere, I smell preteen B.O., my partner is distant, and on from there. Gratitude and "declaring joy" do not shift the trajectory of the thought process. For neurodivergent people, it often feels like we are tricking ourselves. "If everything around me looks miserable, feels miserable, smells miserable, then everything around me IS miserable." I can be thankful for this house and food and still experience misery in my bones. When our nervous system is activated, we will be less likely to progress into a compassionate mindset.

For those of us who internalized an early story of shame and blame, there is the assumption that we are to blame for the misery around us. Raised with dissociative strategies, we may remember moments when our childhood actions caused our parents to be miserable (Remember: the child does not know if they were the cause or not). This internal state will often resonate with the pain we experienced when younger. As an adult looks at the stress in their house, they may simultaneously feel sole responsibility and a childlike sense of "Where is the grown-up in charge?" A parent/caregiver who does not recognize this "inner search for responsibility" may shift the blame to their children, spouse, or other influencing adults within their children's lives. The parent/ caregiver can take on the "parent" role for their own body if they recognize the grief of their neglected younger, inner self. This ownership alleviates a victim shift from occurring. This awareness also allows the parent's nervous system to settle and address the imbalance of stress within the family. Often a child's caregiver will send the message verbally or with body language, "Your emotions are too big for me to navigate!" And a child will shut down. These children grow into adults afraid to experience "drowning" emotions. They then try to protect their children from emotions that previously intimidated their own parents.

As you consider expanding your capacity for grief and joy- you may need support through therapy. Remember: building capacity requires "clearing the path" little bits at a time. To clear the pathway as quickly as possible with chainsaws and stump hogs will allow an immediate release of emotion or energy, but long-term, we do not gain the skills to support trekking down that neural pathway. Dear friends can sit with you and hold space for your grief and joy process. But the goal is not just relief but also long-term strength. It is important to balance "processing" with building internal support. If you received this support as a child, you might not have realized your parent was comforting your grief and building your capacity for resiliency. For example, a child who falls and skins their knee: the parent comforts them, finds a band-aid, then the child skips off and retries riding their bike. The child is learning the pattern of pain, comfort, co-regulation, and confidence to retry. A child who is berated or glared at for falling off their bike, learns that pain is not responded to and giving comfort is uncomfortable for the parent. The child may retry riding the bike - but it is not from a calm nervous system "learning" perspective but to avoid the pain or dismissal from their parent.

One way to re-parent your inner child is by building your capacity for grief. When I was feeling stressed, I would look around for a solution and vocally address the issue to those around me. I was looking for feedback from those in my life, "Did they see how bad it was for me?" But most people did not affirm my distress- my inner self felt increasingly lonely and unseen. The discrepancy between my feeling and other's response caused me to question if I was actually experiencing what was occurring. The disconnect caused me to be louder and more intense as my desperation grew. "Surely, I can't be the only one to see how bad things are! Does no one else feel this way?" Eventually, I realized that it was my internal self feeling desperation. No one external to me could provide the comfort or support - I had to provide that for myself initially.

Tiering my grief (building capacity) looked like this: when I felt angry/sad/annoyed, I chose to stop looking around for external validation but validate myself. Using the self-state perspective, I let my "big self" guide my younger self. "Yes, I see this is so hard and feels so big!" I would write out any patterns I saw - from a bottom-up and C- PTSD perspective - I needed a visual to know I was not "making up" what I experienced. As my younger inner self would express hopelessness, the bigger self did not silence the desperation but provided a safe space to express it. The bigger self would then explain areas of growth the younger self may not be aware of. "I know you did not have anyone to help at 4-years-old, but guess what you did at 16? At 27, you were able to ask for help in such-and-such area." These timelines can help the inner self shift from dissociation into association. As the younger internal self learns to trust the "bigger self" based on its track record and how they have maintained safety and growth- the younger self will reduce its desperation connected to the external environment. I reinforce dissociation and disconnection with myself when I tell the inner part, "Shut up, you are too emotional!" or feed into distress that is "too big for adults".

Caregivers must become adept at navigating grief. Every ounce of grief that is suppressed and rejected does not disappear. As a caregiver disconnects from grief- it finds a place to hide in the body. Weary. Sore muscles. Fogginess. It spreads to everyone in the house. Finding safe spaces to vent, grieve, process, and step into your day is essential. You may think thoughts you have never considered before and hate yourself. Not addressing that grief and pain can lead to resenting the human that reminds you of those thoughts. Hidden sorrow perpetuates pain, shame, and self/other rejection cycles.

I share the following story because I think it is vital for caregivers to understand the depth of their pain and realize, "We are not alone". I sat by the pool several summers ago. All the kids were doing incredible. They were enjoying themselves swimming in the deep end. I still was ever-vigilant, feeling the constant loom of potential stressors- I did not experience "felt safety". At one point, I saw one of my kids doing the "pretend to drown" float thing that some kids do. An intrusive thought swept into my mind: "Would you save them?" I instantly thought, "What??? Yikes, that is awful!" But then my thought process went full circle. I realized the grief I frequently felt with this child's pervasive exhausting struggles. Sitting in this feeling, I realized, "I would save this child because I value life, and they deserve life as much as anyone. But I would hate myself the rest of my life because it could have been easier." Yikes. If you need to put the book down, walk away, take some deep breaths, and process your emotional response to this - go for it. I sat there, stunned by my inner dialogue. I realized how much I wrestled within myself. I regretted putting us in this position. I regretted that life would never be "easy". I regretted that no matter how much acceptance or effort I invested, there would always be a layer of intensity I felt inadequate to handle. These thoughts were shadows hovering behind every interaction. When we view these scary, terrible thoughts in the light of day, they begin to lose their power. Unprocessed, these thoughts are like rocky soil; processed, these thoughts become compost for dramatic change.

In these darkest moments, we must sit with our grief and ugly feelings. We must learn to extend compassion to ourselves, hold the intensity of those emotions, recognize where our body experienced the sensation, and mindfully allow it to be released. Grief is an essential process for a parent. The caregiver must learn how to navigate the grief process like a whitewater rafting tour guide because the family travels those rivers often. The grieving process allows you to feel deeply and then release what may callous into resentment and bitterness. When I see a parent who is vehemently against their children, I see a parent who has not yet learned how to grieve. Grief is: Sitting in the sadness and loss of a moment. Of a painful choice. Of behaviors that may never be "normal". Grieving that you don't think you have all the right tools. Or support system. Or rest. Grieve that your life will never be the same, and it may not be a "blessing." Grieve your relationships pushed to the limit. Grieve the nostalgia for those sweet family moments of before. Grieve that even while they are at school, your stomach is in knots. Grieve that you have lost or gained too much weight because of stress. Grief, when felt in the body, screamed into a pillow, moved through in dance- the depths of grief expand your capacity for joy. You will not force joy by avoiding grief. It is not the nature of these feelings.

Approaching grief with curiosity is to say, "Tell me how it feels in your body. What did you lose? What have you missed? What do you dread?" The safe space then allows compassion to flow. "Ah! Now I see where all these responses are coming from." And with compassion comes connection. Connection to yourself, to what you have cut off. Connection to your partner, kids, and those around you. Then comes the clarity to make more intentional choices- like giving safe space for your children to grieve.

Children who dissociate do so because something they experienced caused them to disconnect. They have experienced loss. They have experienced deep stress. They need a chance to connect and grieve. They need to know their darkest, scariest thoughts will be heard and held as treasures. You can do this once you have learned how to do this for yourself. You will have compassion for what they are experiencing. You will sit with them in the devastating moments, giving them a soft place to land. You will not rush their healing or force behavior changes for the sake of ease. You will help them to see that even in their pain, they are not flawed, just human like the rest of us. Grief opens the door for a positive trajectory. Not grieving prevents all the pieces from hitting the floor; it prevents the brokenness from actually entirely breaking. Grieving enables the process of growth, maturity, and attachment. If the caregiver has walked this path before, they aren't easily offended by the anger and vitriol thrown their way - these are an expression of grief, nothing more than nothing less.

In the compost of grief, gratitude takes root and becomes joy. Not a glib happiness that overlooks pain- but a deep-seated joy that finds space to laugh, dance and enjoy portions of life that we once thought were untouchable. Some questions to reflect on: How does the concept of "grief" feel? What are areas you have had to give up for this current life you are living? What are some parenting choices that you wish could be different? Thinking back to your childhood, what is something you wish could be different? How can you hold that with compassion? What behaviors have you felt are "acceptable" to show grief? What grief behaviors are you uncomfortable with?

Curiosity vs. Rigidity

The growth spiral of expanding grief and joy occurs over a lifetime. Our curiosity is what keeps us engaged with the present. When looking at parenting through a lens of dissociation and embodiment - we must be curious about our histories and the impact on current responses. A nervous system on edge will cling to "rigidity" for stability. Curiosity does not mean the removal of routines or schedules. Curiosity indicates a "safe" nervous system state. When our nervous system is on edge, we may cling to overtly strict policies, nitpick non-essential things, feeling wound up and controlling.

An example is asking my child (ADHD, ODD, PTSD) to get ready in the morning. On a morning when they are on schedule, appear emotionally regulated, and have capacity: If the child has missed part of their morning routine, I will ask, "Please review your mental checklist and see what you are missing." On a morning when they seem rushed, have pressures like a test, and don't seem emotionally regulated: If the child has missed a part of their morning routine, I will say, "Did you take medicine and put on deodorant? Did you take your meds?" I am doing a disservice if I never prompt the child to access their peripheral brain. I am placing additional pressure on the dysregulated child that they may be unable to process if I refuse to shift from my approach.

There is a spectrum of rigidity to curiosity- it is important to recognize where you land and what it symbolizes for your nervous system. As parents, my husband and I have reflected on and modified our approach to the following topics. Take some time to journal or reflect on these questions and concepts. Notice if you feel an openness or a sense of "shutdown" for each topic. Which is one topic you could begin to re-address through a lens of dissociation?

Curiosity for yourself:

Do I, as a parent, disconnect from myself when highly stressed? What does that look like for me? Do I, as a parent, have an activity or pattern for grounding or centering that helps me stay stable? What work have I done to process my own childhood experiences? When I am upset with those in my house, what unreasonable expectations may I have for myself? What interaction helps me feel connected to my kids?

Authority paradigms:

If I, as an adult, continuously center myself, whose story am I focused on? Who do you assume compliance to? Who do you feel you have the right to push back on? Who do you think children should instantly respond to? Who do they not have to listen to? Do you assume "disobedience" is disrespect or a signal of something else? How do you feel inside when someone doesn't listen to you? How were you treated when you didn't comply or listen as a child? Can you think of a time when someone controlled you just because they could? Can you think of a time when someone gave you space to reach your own conclusion/action? How did these two situations differ? When thinking of a stringent caregiver in your life, what justifications do you apply to them? (For example: "My dad was always angry at us for being loud, but he worked hard.") If your child were to think of you, what justifications may they list for you?

Behavior.

Behavior is communication. Many adults read behavior as disruption or inconvenience. Behavior is like waves in the ocean- some are calm, and some are destructive. All waves communicate weather and ocean shifts- they are not "wrong" or "right". Some behaviors are definitely more enjoyable than others! "Good" behavior does not necessarily equal a calm and happy child. Adults who have processed their own history with behaviors will recognize when their children are learning and growing. When a tiny tot is learning how to walk, we don't say, "Oh, you are so clumsy- you fell down!" We know learning to walk requires developing the proper motor and neural skills. As our kids age, they acquire skills in the same process as learning how to walk - the behaviors look drastically different. Instead of wobbling and falling, a child may ruin friendships, be weird, talk back to adults, and even watch inappropriate media. The depth of potential consequences can cause a parent to respond intensely. Embracing the "behavior is communication" mindset allows us to maintain curiosity and compassion towards our children and ourselves. Daily, caregivers unpack these concepts as we view children's behavior through a dissociation lens.

I have heard adults prompt children, "Check your heart because it guides you." This concept sounds like a "self-check". However, the implication is that you will make the right choice and be kind to others if your heart "is in the right place." This assumes moral standing based on a choice; it implies someone is "bad" if they are unkind. If the child IS guarding their heart, by being mean to someone so they can avoid getting hurt first, then they are in line with their "heart". These seemingly innocuous statements from adult experiences disconnect from the experience of a child learning to trust themself. In this situation, a child may pick up on the cue that their behavior still doesn't meet the adult's expectation and learn to adjust. The child may continue in their behavior and internalize, "There is something wrong with my heart." A different approach is to redirect the behavior while reaching to the heart of the matter - "Hey, I noticed you were responding this way- is their a friendship thing I can help you with or do you need to vent about the friend?" Willingness to adapt is a hallmark of brave parenting!

Some questions to reflect on for behavior: Do you know what is developmentally appropriate behavior for the age of your child? Do you allow there to be space for mistakes? Do you assume your child will succeed or fail? Do you believe your child is manipulative or curious? Do you get agitated at the behavior or the response from other adults or authority figures? Think of a behavior that upsets you- now think of a time when someone did that behavior to you. List out the consequences or the repercussions of that moment. Are you expecting that same response from your child? If behavior is communication, what is your child communicating? In your response, what are you communicating? How can you and your child collaborate in problem-solving? Or provide compassion and connection for them to feel safe?

Play:

Our brains are constantly growing and acquiring knowledge through play. Whether playing basketball or with dolls, drawing with chalk or jumping on a trampoline, play encourages growth, connec- tion, and problem-solving. Play is essential. Play can require big muscle movements. Play can require strategic thinking (In our house, we call this strategery. Strategic strategy. Pronounced: Stru-tee-ger-ee). Play can be small and quiet. Play can be individual, interactive, and parallel. Some children find play stressful. They may find the interactions or rules stressful. They may have one eye focused on play and the other eye focused on their caregivers' reactions. Children who have experienced traumas and dissociative splits often struggle with play. The play may seem "off"- not engaged, varied intensity levels, veering from play "norms", and uncertain how to engage. The ANP, responsible for daily functions, may not see the value of play for the child. Due to varied developmental ages, the teenage child may still have the play capacity and goals of a 3-year-old. Neurodivergent individuals often thrive at parallel play and unwatched play. At 39, I prefer parallel play alongside someone doing a puzzle or Dr. Mario than an interactive game. Parents/ caregivers can provide a range of games and play opportunities that different developmental ages of children will enjoy. Emphasizing clear rules, adult supervision, and the opportunity to exit the game early are all strategies that help kids build their play capacity.

Often a child will initiate repair with silliness, imagination, or a game. But the adult will see this silliness as "not taking the issue seriously" or being immature. If an adult can see the invitation of silliness as an invitation to repair the situation and have connection, they are building a solid connection for the future. My kids will do this with jokes, silly would-you-rather questions, and asking to dance. It is beneficial to respect and respond when they advocate from their own inner knowing of the next steps to keep our relationship connected. I silence their self-advocacy and our connection when I do not recognize these connection cues.

Adults deprived of childhood play require play in order to heal. Re-parenting is to "re-parent" our inner self to feel safe and connected. It is just as important to "re-playmate"! If you were a child who was often responsible for the adults around you, if you felt high pressure to "perform perfectly", you can "re-playmate" your younger self! Pick a game or art project - you don't have to be good at it! Feel the uncertainty and anxiety. Let your "bigger self" be a safe space for your "younger self" to make mistakes, make a mess, and feel silly. Reflect on your family's response to play while you were younger. Was play treated as a privilege earned or a necessity? Did your adult play with you? Did your adult laugh with you? Think of a time when play was relaxing. Think of a time when play was stressful. As you grew, how did play shift for you as an adult? When your child plays, do you join in or watch? How do you feel about that? How do you respond if your child breaks the rules of a game? What do you think is causing that shift in their behavior?

Religious and Society Expectations:

Every caregiver has a perspective on acceptable and unacceptable behaviors. It is hard to unpack these perspectives when we view them as "truth" or "unbending". Holding these concepts with an open hand allows us to revisit and clarify what is essential for my family and children's wholeness. Particularly with a lens of dissociation and behavior as communication- if I commit to being offended by some- thing, it better be serious. I will be thoughtful about who I let influence the care of my children. I will recognize that with various parts, my children need a safe space to embody their existence and parts. As adults, we must be diligent not to listen to fears that nefariously impact our parenting. When I say, "Lying is a behavior that exhibits distrust", the response I have heard is, "But it is important for kids not to lie! Lying leads to dishonest people. And society has too many liars." The first reflection question is two-fold: What happens if there are no societal rules - do you trust people actually to trust themselves to do the right thing? Do you trust yourself to do the right thing? Our view of "society falling apart" impacts our ability to curiously respond to a child's current mental framework. That is a lot of pressure for a child to hold. People connected to themselves will make embodied, wise choices on behalf of society. We deflect from holding society accountable by placing individual pressure on children instead of the those in power.

Pick a topic: cussing, kids picking their clothes, types of movies watched, music volume, romantic relationships, clean room, masturbation, etc. Use the following questions to process your approach to the topic: What religious or cultural lens did you grow up with? What was its view on the topic you chose? What was your family's stance? Did that stay the same or shift as you grew older? Assuming your child pushes against that perspective, how do you respond? Are you open to re-evaluating your stance? Why or why not? If it caused your child intense distress, would you choose the societal/religious norm over your child's stability? How does your body feel in public when your child does X? How do you defend them? What is your behavior communicating to them? How can you teach them to respect different rules in different environments?

Failed Expectation vs. Acceptance

One of the greatest gifts we can give our children is to free ourselves from the shame we may experience in parenting someone with intense responses. Another great gift we can give is to release the childhood shame we carry from being an intense child ourselves. A parent who models acceptance of themselves will raise an embodied child who knows themself. If I, as a parent, model that I consistently fail my own expectations and deserve to feel bad, that leads to self-rejection. Self-rejection always leads to other-rejection. If I model that I may fail my expectation but still accept myself regardless, then self-acceptance leads to other-acceptance. We can guide our children in self-acceptance when we accept and align our own big feelings. Our children benefit from consistent expectations and acceptance when they don't achieve. Children need parents to sit in the depth of their feelings to build the confidence to retry. They need validation, "This is a human experience." They can feel big feelings and be rooted to their caregiver simultaneously. Often desperation stems from our belief that we would experience rejection if anyone saw our darkest parts. It is a treasure to hold space for those profound experiences for someone else.

Once we caregivers can grapple with our own trauma histories, responses, parenting philosophies, and grief - we can respond in a way where each human is honored. Here is a scenario recently played out in our house- occasionally, a "win" is wonderful! For several weeks a child had items "appear" at home. She provided vague statements about their origin. I have too many children to be aware of every piece of jewelry they have. I couldn't tell if she was being honest, a self-state was responding, or just blatantly lying. I had not yet confronted her because we had worked hard on trust. I wanted to honor her truth. One day she came home and held out a beautiful pink stone. She said someone had put it on her desk as a surprise, leaving a note that said: "for you". She threw the note away but brought home this beautiful rock. I had a gut feeling the story was bullshit, but I also knew from her demeanor that her eldest self was honestly confused about its origin. I let her ramble on about the rock while internally rolling my eyes at the story and trying to settle myself (I was feeling triggered by stealing- we have a clear expectation about not stealing). "How do we help her repair this and try to build a connection with her internal selves?" was my biggest question. If she is taking things, some parts of her are very overwhelmed. If I assume she stole it and punished her - her internal parts will feed off the distrust.

I asked her to draw out her conference table participants. She drew the rectangle representing the conference table. She drew colored dots around the table to represent different ages. She wrote a little phrase by each colored dot - their respective age/self and their perspective on the rock. When we do this activity, I give space for the child to draw without my interference or questions. As soon as she started drawing, a guilty demeanor covered her face. I looked at her paper, and interestingly, all the self-states were older, 8 to 12-year-old versions of her. It seemed interesting that no younger self-states were appearing.

In my opinion, the "hiding" self-states felt guilty and were avoiding. I asked my child about the self-states that were "hiding". She started to share what she felt in her mind's eye. The youngest self-state had some insight into where the rock came from, but it was still presenting as clueless. I re-explained the purpose of the conference table and thanked the parts for being there. I explained what dissociation can look like with an object appearing. I emphasized that I wasn't accusing her; given our history, it is better to clarify before we assume something is ours. She and I talked, but we knew her other parts were listening. I suggested that if a new object appears - we should confirm with an outside person if it is legit. Even though we will encourage the younger self-states to feel brave and be honest, the eldest self-state can also have a backup plan. I gave the example of something "falling into a purse at the store". If you say, "The item just appeared here, I don't know how!" no one would believe you! Instead, you could say, "I spaced, did I already pay for this?" There are ways to save face, take responsibility, and feel safe. I offered to message her teacher, mention the rock, and make sure he had yet to hear of one missing. If it was actually given to her by someone, she could keep it. She looked relieved and happier after the conversation. In this scenario: I was annoyed that stealing was happening, I was trying to ignore the fears of "what-ifs" for the future, and I wanted her to feel empowered so her self-states would feel comfortable and connected. She did not meet our expectations, but she and her parts deserved acceptance.

A question that my husband and I cycle through is, "Are we always giving in?" What is "too much" nurture? What is "too much" redirecting? When should someone just have consequences? The real world is not this accommodating. We are learning that in these moments of mental swirl, we need to recalibrate, "What are we measuring? What are we teaching? What do we lose by not doing it this way? What do we gain?" Parenting in these situations can be extremely exhausting. In the moments when caregivers desperately need encouragement and support, we may lack the ability to advocate for our selves. When we carry the burden of high-stakes behaviors and responses, it can feel like no one is cutting us slack. My inner critic would chastise my compassion because I was draining my compassion tank on everyone else without giving any to myself. It took me a while to realize that my need for affirmation and encouragement directly correlated to the support I could provide to my children.

Compassion for ourselves, compassion for the child, curiosity towards the situation, and a collaborative effort to resolve these daily irritations create a relationship baseline. Then when something extremely atrocious has occurred, we have already instilled safety and security, giving them a bridge to access alignment. This is especially important when the child has no memory or adamantly denies what has occurred. We waste too many minutes and ounces of energy arguing evidence that supports your situation: Why the child "was" there or why they "are" responsible. We are like prosecutors in a court- room, feeling like there is no relationship without honesty. The reality is that this child may lack internal cohesion, they may not know the facts. If you find yourself feeling like a prosecutor, return to some of the questions from earlier in the chapter. What are you actually responding to? What is the goal at this moment? Are you responding to pressure from other people, your younger self, or your parent at that age? Are you or your child needing more support?

Walking the line of expectations and acceptance can feel like walking a tightrope. I was out of town for a few days of respite. Those days can be rough on the kids due to the change of routine. Often while I get a break, my anxiety builds as I wait for phone calls about my kid's behaviors. I can tell myself, "You don't need to worry", but receiving a call confirms my increasing stress as predictive. It is hard to shift away from an expectation of disruption. Likewise, my kids may associate "mom being gone" with "escalated consequences at school"- while not recognizing the emotional responses involved. A day after I returned, I received a phone call from the Vice Principal. One of my kids had made a poor choice and had to serve a suspension. As I wrestled with my feelings as a parent, I tried to gather up every ounce of curiosity and compassion for when this kid came home from school. He quickly owned up to his part in the situation as we talked. He also explained that he had set a boundary the week before with these kids, reminded them of it earlier in the week, and followed through with it (resulting in a suspension). He is fully responsible for his choices, school consequences, and additional consequences from home. But I also told him I was impressed with his boundaries and how he explained them. This is an essential life skill for a kid that has not had his boundaries respected for most of his life. We discussed involving grown-ups and affirmed that standing up for yourself is very important. We also discussed how other people do not always like the boundary that we set. My son did not meet my expectation of avoiding behaviors that lead to suspension. We maintained connection and acceptance of him by validating and providing redirection for the future. My feelings were simply my feelings. They did not need to impact this situation. My son can make a wise and poor choice in one combination. I can feel irritated and proud of that combination. Two things can be true.

"Those" situations:

What about the really hard, extreme, not changing situations? There will be situations where parents/caregivers have done their due diligence

- parents have gone to therapy, processed their own childhoods, adapted to a connective parenting style, ensured siblings are not bullying/perpetuating harm, and tried medicine and therapy. Yet the child will continue in dysregulation and disruption. The child may have physical or mental needs beyond the current environment and support system; the child may have experienced pains larger than any band-aid in this world can fix. Horrific things can happen, debilitating things can happen, and heartbreaking things can happen.

First, I would like to gently prompt a reflection on how we, as parents, talk about these struggles with others. Parents within "high needs" communities are often treading water, trying to keep themself and their children's heads afloat. Parents try to navigate advocacy for their children and fear that the world won't understand them. Parents are allowed to have feelings and to process them. Parents need to be aware of who they center in their stories. Are we emphasizing my or my family's struggle, or are we shifting the responsibility of blame onto a child? There is a difference between saying, "My adopted kid is driving me crazy, and I can't handle the behaviors." and "I am having such a hard time handling the behaviors in my house. I think it stems from trauma, but I need more support". Or "My autistic kid can't get it together, and we can't go anywhere" vs. "I am sad that our family has to adjust our plans; it feels like I am missing out." We place a disproportionate power on the child's shoulders if they are centered as the core source of a family's stress. The child who shoulders the power to "destroy a family" is growing up with a high shame, high blame experience. They are subsequently the victim of AND responsible for every harm. The tendency to blame the child often reflects an adult who held a disproportionate responsibility for the stability of their own family of origin. Some children do need extensive support systems for their entire life. This reality is heartbreaking and complex. But the caregiver's needs can be spliced from the child's needs.

Sometimes parents find themselves re-traumatized by their children. It is almost as if the traumatized younger self-state of the child is reaching out to the traumatized younger self-state of the parent. Children assert self-protection through avoidance, dominance, and assimilation. A child (who has experienced substantial abuse and has internal self- states due to dissociation) may sense a "fractured part" of the adult. The child and adult are often unaware of this dynamic. These adults may feel violated or highly anxious around these children. The child may feel the fear or violation of the adult's internal younger self. When the child (or the child's ANP) senses this dynamic and sees the adult behaving uneasily or anxious around them, the child will make a choice leading to self-preservation. Adults who are aware of their own history and have helped their internal younger self to feel safe can redirect the child's younger self towards self-attachment.

Understanding the role of inner parts in extreme behaviors provides a vital lens for how we respond. The following examples intend to demonstrate how internal parts respond within these problematic situations. At times a child who has experienced sexual abuse may sense the caregiver or adult's inner self who also experienced abuse. It is like the ANP of the adult and the ANP of the child are trying to determine safety. As a child's ANP may feel the fear and uncertainty building, they will be unable to maintain daily functions in this heightened stress state. They may initiate an act in order to get their nervous system to step out of "hyper-vigilance". The child is not consciously choosing "I will initiate", but is responding to the protective "magnetic vibe".

Another example is physical violence- the child's inner part will prompt the adult to harm them. The child's ANP can then return to "functioning". This is why some children appear relieved or calm after a harmful encounter. Their system is re-regulating. Some children will choose avoidance - this is not always a conscious choice but a strategy that protected their earlier age during trauma. Sometimes an action will not occur, but there is a "vibe" or energy-sensation emitted from the EP's trauma history. A child's EP may alert the child to a danger that is not currently existing, this feeds into the dynamic of suspicion and distrust. An example is the child waking up and coming down for breakfast. Caregiver says, "Good Morning!" and walks over to pat their arm. The child's inner EP sends off a warning signal "danger!" The child may not consciously connect this internal warning, but may shift in behavior and become vigilant. The adult may sense a shift in response and wonder why the child is avoidant at breakfast.

If adults are highly aware of their own internal self, they can recognize when the child has shifted from their current age to a different self-state. The adult can recognize when a child is dysregulated and scanning for unsafety. The adult can then choose to give space, not be affectionate, or make choices that maintain safety for the child and themself. A home with children trying to navigate dissociative parts or an adult disconnected from their inner self can perpetuate additional harm. In a home where the adults are connected to their inner self and all children have support - these "vibes" can be an insight into the EPs and the harm they are trying to process from young, nonverbal ages.

A child previously placed in a caregiver role will often be scanning for "weakness" or "inadequacy" of the caregiver/parent. In my experience, this can look like a child "testing" your competence with nonstop requests. Or the child is criticizing parenting decisions or hovering over the other kids. This vigilance is typical during transitions to a new home with a child from foster care. It is healthy to be vigilant in the home of a stranger! This vigilance can be "re-traumatizing" if the adult was also a caregiver-child. If the adult feels constantly undermined, they will misunderstand the child's communication. The child will see red flags of dominance if the adult tries to assert their "authority" position. If the adult recognizes that the child needs a "felt sense of safety," they will include the child in a balance of adult and child activities. For example, letting the child help plan some meals or put away groceries (so they know what food is available), let them pack a lunch for a younger sibling (continue in their quasi-caretaker role), and then have them go on an individual outing with a friend (be a kid and play). The child can then begin to develop trust for the adult providing and caring for siblings, and they can experience some fun while also developing the neural pathways that "my siblings will be safe while I am gone". To force a caregiver-child into a "just a child" role too quickly can lead to too much internal distress.

There are many more extreme scenarios. Violence, harm, and heartbreak. In these challenging situations, caregivers may need to "redefine" their relationship with the child until there can be fluent safety and acceptance. It may be wise to set a mental boundary of "I will be a safe, neutral grown-up", not "I'm a mom expecting reciprocal affection or bonding". Mentally relabelling a relationship can shift our expectations for ourselves and/or the child. This shift decreases pressure for connection, performance, and attachment. Over time this process can evolve into a child/parent connection. And if it does not develop into a child/parent connection- you have chosen to model and insist on safety. You have chosen connective strategies that do impact their neural capacity for future relationship connections. You have maintained a compassionate connection to your own humanity.

8

Sibling Interactions

As I write this, our family is stable and our five kids get along as well as most siblings. Yet I feel uncertain - what would a "successful sibling relationship" look like? How do I know we have "done the right things"? I recognize that as the parent, it feels out-of-my-control for these humans to create their own paths in the world and forge their own relationships. I will share things in this chapter that will help sibling and peer relationships- yet I also know my own kids are not fully grown up. There is no shiny bow at the end of this story - we still have our lifetimes to live out these relationships. The hovering parenting question is, "Did I screw up my kids?" But I also know that at some point, we become responsible for our own choices.

Here are some truths that I find helpful to remind myself: Children are humans who are learning and growing. Children do not have to like or enjoy being around certain people. Children can have preferences. Children will have different perspectives of events than adults or peers. Children can have awful days. Children deserve to feel safe. Children have the right to be treated safely. Children with dissociated parts deserve to feel safe. As the caregiver: I am responsible for maintaining a safe environment. I can not remove discomfort or tension for my child. I can assist at the level they need to be supported. I am not responsible for every choice they make. I may get along with one child's personality more than another, which does not make them a favorite. I am responsible for finding ways of connecting with personalities I do not traditionally get along with. Everyone can be their own person.

Family dynamics are tricky because you have different people with different opinions, preferences, personalities, and choices. Sibling dynamics are tricky because you have people with different opinions, preferences, personalities, and choices - also being instructed by adults with their own thoughts, opinions, and personalities. From "what to eat for breakfast" to "what defines a clean room" to school work expectations, there are plenty of opportunities for disagreement. Adding in diagnoses and/or disabilities to the mix, there are new layers of expectation, support, and emotions. If your family formed through foster care or adoption- there are additional layers of different lived experiences, separate traumas, shared traumas, and goals of connection. A dissociation lens views sibling and family interactions as impacted by the potential inner parts of the child. Instead of my family with five kids, I may have five physical kids- and multiple inner parts to be aware of at any given time. This sounds complicated - however, using the dissociation lens provided insight that helped diminish miscommunication and disruptions between siblings. Instead of rehashing the same arguments or complex scenarios, we empower the kids to have curiosity and compassion while setting boundaries. This chapter will address transference of adult sibling experience, triangulation, fair vs. equal, honoring each perspective, being your own individual, trauma bonds, boundaries, and safety. These concepts helped provide a foundation for our kids to have "felt safety" and positive interactions with each other.

-Transference of Adult Sibling Experiences

It is normal to see a reflection of ourselves in our children. Whether shared eye color or personality style- these similarities can bring a feeling of connection and warmth. Sometimes shared characteristics are a source of fear and concern. When I look at my daughter, I see many personality characteristics that are similar to mine- I resonate with her intensity and silliness. I also have wounds from when I was "too much" for other people. As I parent her, I often catch myself wanting to advise her on how to "play it safe"- which is a reflection of my own rejections and need for safety. When our children squabble and the youngest is left out, my husband (the youngest child) feels that loneliness intensely while also realizing how he may have been overzealous as the youngest child. Connecting to the commonality we share with a child is positive, but we should remember that the child is not us.

Caregivers must recognize when a healthy shared characteristic becomes an isolating or dangerous barrier that keeps others at a distance. Using eye color as an example: My spouse has blue eyes, one of our kids has blue eyes, another has gray/chameleon eyes, and three have brown eyes similar to mine. The blue-eyed child has frequently heard, "You have gorgeous blue eyes just like your dad!" The gray or chameleon (changes hue based on clothes) eye child has eyes like two of their grandparents, "Your eyes are so unique! They look just like Grandpa and Nannie's!" It is less frequent for someone to be captivated by the rich chocolatey tones of our brown eyes. My three children, various brown hues of their irises, are often seen for their skin color- their eyes, "Of course you have brown eyes." A healthy-shared characteristic can become an isolating barrier keeping others at a distance. If I, as an adult, make these comments - What is my goal? If my goal is connection, will I find areas of commonality with each child? What biases are behind my statements? Is there a moment from my child- hood when I was the "preferred" child or the "pushed away" child? What can I connect to in each child? Some children, removed from their homes of origin, will have conflicting feelings about shared characteristics with their biological families. When I see that resistance, I try to find more distant ancestors for the child to feel a connection. Belonging is vital. Children with ANP and EPs may experience more heightened conflicts of belonging. Finding a connection that is valuable to them will strengthen their internal belonging.

Caregivers who process our experiences - including relationships with siblings, the parent-sibling triangle, physical characteristics, and our personality styles- will respond to sibling interactions in a balanced way. If I experienced abuse from a sibling, I might be hyper-vigilant about certain characteristics or red flags in my children. Caregivers who do not reflect may over-support one child and punish or reject the other. If my parent always preferred one of my siblings, I may push away one of my kids who reminds me of them. Or I may overly con- nect with them- as my inner child may see safety in that relationship. A parent who has not reflected on their own internal parts may feel a heightened sense of insecurity and fear around their children with dissociation. If an adult's inner child feels unsafe, they may instigate negative interactions with their own child. Without a dissociation lens, the caregiver may try to change these behaviors - but without the inner child experiencing connection, the behaviors will continue because the "felt safety" does not exist. Changing the trajectory of intergenerational trauma requires addressing our past and present so that we can address the future differently.

Triangulation is when two people connect over the angst of another person. Each person is a point on the triangle. The relationships can shift- two siding against the other. This can happen with siblings and between siblings and parents. For a child who experienced a dissociative shift, the ANP will use triangulation as a survival strategy. They may see other kids playing happily, walk over, ask the perfect question to cause disruption, and then walk away. The ANP and the child are two points on the triangle against the other person. The child and ANP will ex- perience emotional relief by watching the other person sift through the chaos. This pattern continued into adulthood contributes to a pattern of ruptured relationships and isolation of the person. Instead, the child and ANP need support to process their feelings of jealousy or rejection. Support to process challenging feelings can shift the triangulation into a proactive, accountable self.

Triangulation can also inadvertently happen when a child tells on another child. If the child shares the situation and the stress, and the parent "sides" with the child- it can become "them" against another child. With a large household, I will not even realize that triangles have formed between siblings or adults. Our current strategy is to address this head-on. We normalize that siblings will go through seasons where they feel closer to one than another. We reaffirm our expectations for treating each other decent. And I increase my observation to see what is instigating the triangulation. I shift my role as the parent - instead of swooping in to help, I will encourage the children to address situations with each other. Sometimes this requires adult help to mediate. If I see a child causing chaos, I will prompt them to process hard feelings with me, encouraging their self-trust instead of chaos bombing. These patterns of triangulation may have occurred within our own homes of origin. The caregiver can reflect on their experiences and their role in the triangle.

-What is the goal?

Sometimes my goal is for all the kids to co-exist peacefully. Other times, the goal is for them to play with each other for over 35 minutes without an argument. Occasionally the goal is for everyone to be on their tablets or game systems while I'm assisting a dysregulated child. When our family was merging two sets of siblings, the goal was for the kids to learn about each other and create shared spaces within the house. A temporary triage goal is okay. But be careful if a triage goal becomes an ongoing permanent response. For example, when my kids were 2-year-olds, they were expected to be in a stroller or holding my hand while we walked in a public space. Assuming "typical" developmental growth, I don't require my 12-year-old to hold my hand in public. Goals can and should change over time. The following scenario played out well over a year, causing daily stress - until we learned how to identify the need and set an appropriate goal. Goals can look different for every child. In a safe environment, children can see the benefit of individual goals and understand it is not a competition.

I sent five kids outside to play in the backyard. They all begin to play tag. After 15 minutes, arguing begins. Arguing lasts for 10 minutes.

Eventually, children scatter; some still play tag, and others do their own thing. A child opens the backdoor to announce the "game failed". Three minutes later, a different child opens the backdoor to tell on someone. Thirty seconds later, another child "needs some water". One minute later, another child needs water. My original goal was for kids to be outside of the house playing. My initial goal focused on my sensory overwhelm and needing a break from all the sounds. The sounds of arguing from outside and the constant interruptions did not help me work towards accomplishing my goal of a "break".

We tried a variety of strategies - having the kids need to work it out themself before getting me, having them rotate who was "in charge" of the game, removing people from the game, and putting a water canteen outside with cups. These did not shift the arguing and the limited play-ing time. Sometimes it felt like people were more agitated after playing than before. I chose to sit and watch the interactions to figure out where the system was breaking down. First, I realized that two of the primary children were struggling due to how their brains function. The Autistic child needed predictability in the game, the pattern of turn-taking, the routine of paths, clarity of rules, and the fun part of being chased. The ADHD kiddo needed a dopamine surge to maintain interaction in the game, a clarity of transition between "taggers", and a way to "escape" from the game without getting in trouble. At 10 minutes, this child would ask others to change the game (add a monster character, different routes, etc.). This "ask" began the argument spiral. Second, I observed how when chased, some kids would make highly impulsive, unsafe choices to avoid getting tagged - jumping unsafely off a high place, running into things, etc. The dysregulation showed a heightened adrenaline surge with a reduced "calculated" approach. In our house, I encourage exploring behaviors - but there must be a calculation and safety in how you play, where you play, and the level of intensity. The activity is not necessarily dangerous, but how we approach it may be dangerous. Third, I saw that the kids felt they had to pick sides. Should they side with the kid who needed routine or the kid who wanted to play differently? Should they tell on the kid playing dangerously? Did they even want to play anymore? Fourth, I saw that coming in and getting water was a form of self-regulation. They were looking for adult feedback and a chance to cool off to get a break from the arguing and intensity.

Reflection: After reading this scenario- what patterns or thoughts catch your eye? Do you relate to this experience? Do you relate to one of the children's experiences? What is a short-term goal? What is a long-term goal? What is your parent/caregiver goal? What are the barriers to these goals? Do you feel resistance to this idea?

I addressed this situation by focusing on adult presence, ways to leave the game peacefully, and supporting the two kids with the most pressing concerns. I did not want to be present. I wanted a break and needed space. But I knew I would not get that if I shut the door. It was worth it, in the long run, to be visible. I took my coffee and book outside. The visible presence of an adult reduced the level of desperation in behavior. Trauma in the early years impacts a child's critical developmental stages of trust and connection. A 9-year-old may have the social skills to navigate the game of tag, but a 1.5-year-old "younger self" will need external support to check-in with their adult. [Picture a toddler running around the yard but looking back at the parent to verify they are in the acceptable zone or have crossed out of a boundary. This is normal development for a young child; an older child seeking that affirmation can look disruptive.]

The kids and I discussed ways to leave a game if they are overwhelmed and need a break. We also discussed how different brains work. We did not act shocked when the predictable request for a "change of rules" occurred. Instead, I would prompt, "X needs the game consistent, and Y wants a change. Is there a way we can do both or let someone know what time we can switch?" The kids started to learn to say, "In 5 minutes, can we play a different version?" It gave a predictable warning that some children needed. By providing safe ways to leave the game- they did not feel they needed to tell on each other or pick sides.

The child who had the most disruptive behaviors began to learn that they could exit gracefully instead of chaotically. Adult presence helped regulate feelings of disappointment, which we experience when a game ends or we do not get the desired result.

This process required intentional time upfront. Over months we practiced these skills. Once the kids saw they could safely have a say in the game rules, there were more moments of frustration when kids tested out variations of tag and ways to escape the game. Bottom-up thinkers often have to re-enact these scenarios in various approaches to see what works and what does not. The child with C-PTSD may not realize that they have a say and will continue to go along with the other kids until months later when they realize that they too can suggest ideas! For the extra resistant child, I reduced their playtime so they could end successfully. Before they began arguing, I would ask them to come in for a drink and ask about the fun parts of playing. Giving them a break before they recognized they needed a break was vital in changing the impulsivity pattern to escape. Building their confidence helps them find ways to connect and play positively with their peers. It also allowed the child and me to shift the behavior/consequences cycle.

Think of one goal. Get curious- Do the siblings have the same goal as you, the caregiver? What was your childhood experience with this goal? What do you see as steps to reach a long-term goal? *Have compassion-* This will not change overnight. These patterns have been in place for a long-time. Show compassion for what your kids are experiencing and what you or your partner feel. Be connected- Are you connected to yourself? Can you let yourself feel an emotion with- out judgment? Can you reach out to a friend or family for help or support? What is a positive way you are connecting to the child currently? Connection is not a reward. What can you overlook to focus on connection as a building block? *Cultivate with Intention-* Remember your goal while responding to sibling interactions. Overlook what is not an emergency and is not necessary to this phase of the goal. Encourage micro-skill behaviors. Celebrate yourself for parenting in a kind and supportive way.

-Fairness

The universal cry, "This is not fair!!!!", is heard in every family, class-room, and playground. It does not matter the formation of your family. This issue is important for children to learn to navigate. "Fairness" stirs up big feelings that flood us grown-ups; of course, it will flood our kids. In a home with foster children - there will be questions of fairness. In a home with adopted children - there will be questions of fairness. In a home with biological children - there will be questions of fairness. In a home with zero diagnoses - there will be questions of fairness. In a home with many diagnoses - there will be questions of fairness. When you hear someone questioning "fairness", is your gut reaction "You get what you get, and you don't throw a fit"? Do you hear "ungratefulness"? Do you hear a question of belonging and connection? Do you hear a concern or a demand? Do you picture specific environments that do not have space for fairness? Is the child expressing, "I want more" or "I want to know how I fit in this place"? Wrestling with fair vs. equal will empower you to navigate your child"s processing of fair vs. equal. This can impact rewards, consequences, privileges, and how your household responds to behaviors.

Once you have reflected on your own experiences with fairness, have conversations surrounding "fairness" with your kids. Using clothing as an example, in our family we make sure each child has essentials (socks, underwear, tops, and bottoms). If one child has a hole in a shirt, I will replace that shirt, but I won't replace everyone's (this is fair, not equal). If a child intentionally keeps destroying clothing, we will determine what is distressing and how to help them build responsibility. If a child wants $300 Jordans or a specific style, they can save up their allowance and purchase those items. Clothing was an easy object lesson in demonstrating fair/equal to our kids. Some of our kids like footie pj's, others can not stand them! If I were equal, I would give everyone the same pajamas. If I am fair, I will respect the difference in preference and texture.

Children with different diagnoses will require different levels of support from their parents- different approaches to consequences, rewards, and follow-through. At first, this can look highly unfair. The bottom-up processing child will need micro-supports and reinforcement throughout the day. Another child may accomplish the task without guidance. Do I reward the child who completed the entire task without support? Do I reward each micro-accomplishment of the child needing extra support? If a child has several different aged inner self-states, with different developmental milestones - which gets rewarded, affirmed, or a consequence? As caregivers, we need to decide what are our foundational expectations. Then reflect on your children - their development, history, and what is a reasonable expectation for them. Normalize that different people sharing the same household will have different goals. For example, if "respect for personal space" is an expectation for our house, I will hold everyone to that expectation but have different pacing for each person. A dissociative strategy is to say, "Stay out of their bubble!" A connective approach recognizes the gap between expectation and performance. One child respects physical space but not auditory space- so we focus on sounds. Another child needs to "bump into things" for stimulation, so we work on filling that sensory input instead of saying, "Respect someone's space". Another child "accidentally" touches people, so we work on "intentionally" placing ourselves away from others. Children whose needs are respected learn to treat others fairly. They know how to advocate for their needs instead of assimilating into a societal norm.

The framework of authority, consequences, and immediate performance needs to create more space for learning at the pace of development. This framework causes children to see each other as liabilities, not assets. High consequence, low modeling households will reinforce dissociative strategies. This may look like compliance or "peace" in the short term but does not develop a connected child. The framework of curiosity, compassion, and connection leads to environments that cultivate peace and self-awareness. These children look out for the best for each other and ways to support their individual needs. A great way to explore your family setup is to ask! We revisit the "fairness" issue several times yearly - they can write issues down or talk to us. Sometimes kids need explanations of the "why" behind a parent's choice. Sometimes, they see a need in a sibling or themself that their parents don't see. Sometimes kids need space to say, "We need more affirmation or encouragement". Sometimes I will ask them to suggest resolutions to a situation or problematic pattern. Kids who feel they have a voice in the family are less likely to lash out at other kids. Kids who feel secure will ensure other children also experience security.

One topic we discuss is how fairness is different depending on the environment. For example, in our house, the kids decide when to complete their chores and shower, fitting into the family schedule. At home, we give a 5-minute warning before they must be off their video games or media. The environment may require a faster response time at school or on a sports team. Schools are supposed to meet the learning needs of each student, but they require structures and rules for taking care of large groups of children. A child with dissociated parts may experience a heightened "unfairness" meter. Their life has already experienced a deficit with high levels of unfairness. I would buy 5 of each seasonal item (glowing reindeer noses at Christmas, Easter bubbles, and Halloween flashlights)- one for each child. Consistently, my eldest child's item would not work. The light would stop glowing, the object would crack, or the battery would die. These were not big deal items, but to a child who had experienced much unfairness, her inner self believed this was intentional. For a while, I bought extras to ensure she and her internal parts knew they had plenty. Then we could navigate situations where there were not enough items or items broke. It takes time and skill-building to navigate fair vs. equal.

-Be a detective
Misreading body language and misunderstanding intent often contribute to relational breakdowns. Most of my neurodivergent kiddos

are not well-versed in body language or "reading a room". My kiddos with trauma backgrounds may over-analyze other people's body language and experience disconnection from their own responses. The ANP can be a great partner to help the child learn clues for navigating their internal shifting and relationships with others. We encourage each child to be a detective. Look for body language clues, context clues, or auditory clues. Look for body signals your own body is sending- "Does your belly feel weird or shoulders tight?, Does your body feel calm and unclenched?" If a child feels dysregulated, then their self-states may tend to shift more rapidly, causing a higher level of dysregulation for themself and confusion for others.

One of our kids was having a rough time at school, they got along with a few people but got caught up in drama with most kids in the class. Every day after school, this smiling child would bound off the bus with a list of negative interactions with peers. They did have a few friends. I asked what she liked about them. I realized the common factor with those kids is that they were "easy to read". This child did not have to read between the lines with them. The friends would tell this child if they stepped out of line. They didn't talk about this child to others. It was a safe relationship that involved easy-to-understand cues. The other kids (and probably this child) were sending mixed signals, acting like friends but shifting in their interactions. This child was wary of even positive interactions. In school, they were learning about clouds, so I used the metaphor of clouds to explain the patterns. Some kids are "clear day" kids - what you see is what you get. You feel good around them. You can understand them. "Cloudy day" kids are a bit more complicated. You may feel good around them sometimes, and other times you feel lousy around them. It is hard to know when they are with you or against you. Sometimes people are also "thunder- storms"; if you keep standing near their lightning, you will get hit every time. We then shifted the conversation from others to personal. Was she acting in a "clear day", "cloudy day", or "thunderstorm" way? Often attempts to "keep up with conversation" would leave them saying things they quickly regretted, making more enemies than friends. Though I love sarcasm and a good joke, we have shifted the approach in our house to become "clear day" people. Teaching our kids strategies to understand other individuals' body language and intent is important. It is a long-term benefit for them to learn how to present them- selves and their intent as clearly as possible.

Whether from anger or a sensory input need, a family may have one child who is more aggressive than the others. This child can un-intentionally use their communication to alienate or provoke everyone else. Others quickly learn not to "awaken the beast". A parent may view this child as just needing more space; however, they probably also need space to process their frustrations with the current family dynamic. Our child who explodes the most easily and is constantly telling on others- was seemingly impossible to calm down. This child has a high value on safety and justice. I could see their frustration at people not following the rules or acting "out of line" was based on the feeling that everyone was out of control. I started to interpret for him, "I know it sounds like he is angry at you, but he is concerned that you aren't being safe for yourself, and he wants you to be safe." The other kids began not to feel verbally attacked. The child could see their goodness underneath the anger. The presentation needs to improve, but the intent is good. A "justice-loving" child will feel the tension in a family and seek stability by trying to silence those causing disruption. It is beneficial to help them see the growth process and understand how the brain works. They can join the process if they know what the family is working towards (for example, cohesion and compassion).

"Being a detective" can shift a reactionary hyper-vigilance into self-aware stability. Children who do not recognize patterns with social cues and relationships subconsciously pick up on patterns that influence our bodily responses. For example, a child's shoulders tense whenever they hear stomping feet. Over time they may tense up at all loud feet- even if nothing negative happens. They go into "shadow" mode, avoiding interacting with the person who stomped. This pattern (stomping feet:

tense shoulders: avoiding person) happens so frequently that they connect the stimulus and response only when they are adults. If a child is encouraged to express when they feel unsettled, it can change stress absorption. Parenting with a dissociative lens means encouraging our kids to express discomfort as self-advocacy.

At the beginning of this skill development, it may look like the child over-complains or over-recognizes discomfort. Affirm their discomfort or acknowledge what they recognize. Remember that the child may share a clue that a dissociative part recognizes. Over time we shift from "noticing" to embodying our experience and advocating for a boundary. In a sibling relationship, one child may notice they feel on edge around another. A child may be hyper-vigilant, walking on eggshells, and over-reactive when the other kid is around. To be a detective, the child could recognize their stomach feels jumbled when they see this sibling: if the sibling is chaotic (frantic movements, nonstop talking), "I feel on edge", and if the sibling is reading (calm, still), "I feel I can approach them".

Being a detective, includes recognizing our own reactions! If other kids are unpredictable, can I know I am acting in the best way for me? For several years one of our kids would scream a level 10 scream regardless if someone looked at them wrong or they were hurt. There was no way to tell the difference. Siblings would attempt to check if they were okay, often putting themself in the fire of this child's explosion. When the behavior was new, I would run over, quickly assessing and separating the kids. That set the pattern of "when I scream, mom comes running". Each child's expression would shift every time there was a scream. Some kids were angry, and others assumed they were to blame- even if no fault had occurred. Reteaching a child to use a scream scale from 1-10, no big deal to worst possible, was necessary so the other kids were not living in perpetual fear of getting in trouble. We also had to prompt the other kids to check in on themself- "Did I do anything to that sibling?" If the answer was no, then go about your business.

-Boundaries

An empowered child is given the vocabulary for and encouraged to set boundaries. A safe child knows they can express a preference or a dislike and still be accepted and valued. A respected child is allowed to have good days and bad days. A child securely attached to themself will learn how to connect but not enmesh with others. A child securely attached to a caregiver will learn that expressing big feelings can be done in a way that values both participants. Many of us adults are learning about boundaries alongside our children. This may require verbalizing to your child, "I am still trying to figure this out myself!" and exploring together what makes sense and feels right. Unboundaried parenting sends the message that "You belong to me. Based on my emotional roller coaster, I can invade your space and revoke your rights anytime." Boundaried parenting sends the message, "There is intentionality behind our decisions. You exist in your personhood. Our choices and emotions impact each other. We each have a right to feel them, but we will respect the connection within this family."

Reflection: Did you grow up with boundaried or unboundaried parenting? What rights did the children have? Did you observe your parents set boundaries with other adults?

Teaching our kids to have boundaries encourages their self- awareness. All children benefit from this. Children who have experienced trauma and had their boundaries violated must practice boundary setting in a safe environment that maintains a connection. Children with dissociated parts will need developmentally appropriate ways to practice asserting their boundaries - physically and communicatively. Children with high oppositional behaviors often have a deficit in boundary reciprocity. When we can increase their self-advocacy, we can often diminish oppositional behaviors. An additional note: when children are learning boundaries, expect them to assert in the wrong way, at the wrong time, about something that does not seem necessary. Like other learned skills, finding the right balance takes practice and testing.

Caregivers can ask questions and can compromise. "I am curious about this boundary, and what about it feels important to you?" "I appreciate you do not want to wear socks with your Crocs because they squish your feet. It is 12 degrees out, and I need your toes to be warm. Is there a way I can support your preference and also maintain my pro-sock stance?" If I view every assertion of boundary as a threat to my parenting or my authority, that is a "me" issue that I need to process as a caregiver. If I view these as learning opportunities that build self- awareness and independence, I can respect the process without feeling threatened. Siblings who are allowed to have boundaries will also be siblings who feel connected and valued by each other. Siblings who experience violated boundaries will violate the boundaries of each other.

In our house, we recognize that a child with various mental health struggles, addictive tendencies, high sensory needs, and memories/ experiences that haunt them, has a higher chance of engaging in risky behaviors, including substance abuse. This risk does not diminish the child's right to exist or be accepted. On a large, future scale, setting a foundation for acceptance, self-accountability, and boundaries for other kids is valuable. You can love someone and not be able to fix or help them. That is heartbreaking and a reality. We recognized some family patterns could contribute to this pipeline- and wanted to address them while the kids were younger. One of these patterns is when a child feels untethered to their emotions- they may seek the pushback of someone else in order to experience a tangible boundary. They do not know how to articulate, "I am feeling out of control and need someone to help me limit myself." We wanted to make it clear in our house: You, as a child, are not responsible for providing boundaries for another child or an adult. Ever. You are only responsible for labeling your own boundaries.

Here is an example from playing tetherball as a family: Two kids would play tetherball - there was a rhythm and settledness to the intensity. One child began to play aggressively - slamming the ball, crossing the court line, and grabbing the string. The other child is caught off guard by the shift and attempts to match the energy. The second child finally explodes, "You are playing unfairly. That's against the rules! I hate you!" The first child responds, "You don't know how to play the game.

I'm following the rules! I didn't touch the ball on your side." The second child is confused and angry. The second child's pushing back prompts the first child's energy to return to a contained space. The second child stomps away, swearing never to play together again.

You could sit the first child down, draw a chart of the interaction and show them how they caused the chaos. This does not work- I've tried. When the first child's emotions spiral (EP), their nervous system is dysregulated. They can only problem-solve once they are back to base-line. The ANP is concerned about their child. Caring about the second child's well-being is not within their job description. We began to teach the kids to name their boundaries and follow the best path for them-self. It is not conducive to debate with a dysregulated nervous system. The second child learned to say, "I will continue to play if we follow the rhythmic play of before. I will not play if it becomes aggressive." They can assert their boundary without serving as a boundary for the other child.

If a child cannot interact reciprocally, the other children need a plan to preserve the relationship before it fully deteriorates. It took us a lot of trial and error to get to the point where our children could learn to disengage in a way that honored both individuals involved. We wanted the kids to know that getting a grown-up for help is important, but you also have the power to step away from a relational interaction that does not serve both parties. It is how you value relationships. We model these interactions and step in to help give vocabulary and cue turn-taking dialogue. Now that we recognize how these shifts are related to differ-ing self-states, it is even more valuable that rejections are not occurring but relationship preservation. I may prompt a child, "Wow! Seems that you feel very frustrated! You can say, 'I love playing with you when we both feel safe, and I will be happy to play with you when we can feel connected." I then emphasize, "This is how we value you and him - sometimes valuing a relationship means giving a safe space for them to settle". I want the other child and any self-state listening to know that it is not a rejection but a preservation.

-Trauma Bonds

Trauma bonds are connections formed from trauma that result in self-blame. In her book, "Set Boundaries, Find Peace", Nedra Glover Tawwab explains, "Physical abuse and emotional abuse are boundary violations. When people are unaware that this type of treatment is wrong, they may view abuse as an expected part of a relationship... When victims start to believe they are responsible for their abuse, or when they start to sympathize with the perpetrator, trauma bonding occurs. Trauma bonding limits our ability to set boundaries because we think we're the cause of the perpetrator's actions. People who grew up in abusive homes have a higher likelihood of developing trauma bonds later in life. Also, the longer the abusive relationship continues, the harder it is to leave. Trauma bonding happens in families where children believe that they are responsible for what is said and done to them."

In a household where the caregivers are changing intergenerational trauma patterns, the caregiver can focus on boundaries. A caregiver who reclaims responsibility for dysfunction will remove a burden of responsibility from the child. A caregiver who sets boundaries around their choices and responses can assert, "This is an adult issue to resolve", instead of shifting blame to the child. Narrating the caregiver experience can provide clarifying information for the child and their inner parts. An example is when I was in elementary school. My mom was driving my brother home in our maroon minivan. He asked for a cassette tape, and as she drove, eyes straight ahead, she reached for the cassettes. The case fell over, and reflexively, Mom looked down to grab what had fallen. In that split second of looking away, she veered and drove into a car parked on the street. Now, she was only going 15 mph in the neighborhood, and no significant damage was done. The car's owner was annoyed, and we had this story about "when the cassettes fell". My mom emphasized the importance of keeping her eyes on the road. She explained that when we were old enough to drive, we should wait until the car is stopped to look down. Mom set a boundary around her choice, claimed ownership, and narrated what had occurred in a non-blaming way. She did not blame the child for the falling tapes, the car crash, or her emotions. Mom was not treated this way as a child but was determined to shift the power dynamic positively.

In a household where siblings have shared trauma- they may experience their inner parts having trauma bonds that their current age does not experience. For example, two children did not consistently have food between the ages of 1 and 3. As 12 and 13-year-olds, their current environment has plenty of food. Sometimes when dinner time arrives, the two kids will be angry at each other, arguing about food and staring competitively. Their vibe differs from "goofing off"; the interaction has a survival edge. Another indicator of a dissociative shift is when we give redirection instructions, and the child thinks it is brand-new information. There is resistance to change and acting "clueless" at what is said. We can remind them that there is plenty of food, but the youngest internal parts, ages 1 and 3, need more co-regulation than a verbal reminder. The kids may need pairing with an adult or non-trauma-bonded sibling who can safely body double eating. The children may also feel unnerved by the flood of stress they experience and need help reintegrating into the family after a dissociative episode.

These are some examples of how trauma bonds can show up in sibling relationships: survival competition (only one of us can survive), the scapegoat (one child takes on the brunt of negativity), dominance (the child who feels oppressed takes out their aggression on another as a form of "processing"), displacement of tension (a dysregulated state that shifts tension on to another person so I can feel calmer), protection and rejection (sibling will be very protective of another sibling, but then also keep them distant). The caregiver should reflect on their own experiences with these topics first. Then consider your children: their experiences, the trauma bonds they may experience, consistent times this shows up (transitions, bedtime, eating, etc.), can you co-regulate with them, and how to comfort and not punish trauma-based sibling interactions.

After homeschooling one of my children, I felt I was supposed to keep an additional child at home the following year. I knew she needed to catch up on some academics while building her emotional capacity. The two kids had been home for two days without the other three interfering for the first time. These two had different dissociation levels and a constantly activated trauma bond. Chaos unfolded anytime I left the room. Initially, I tried working on their strategies for interacting. Separated them into different rooms and placed them in "penalty zones" within the same room. One day I had them working in different rooms. I went in to check, and he was muttering to himself, "She called me a b****. I hate her." Our house is not strict with language, but the child he referred to never uses cuss words. Ever. She even put a sign on her bedroom door "Club: boy-free zone. Cuss-free zone". I asked him what she had said and how did he know? He said that he saw her lips moving and that she said it whenever she saw him. Knowing what I knew then about his paranoia, I knew that he was inaccurate in his interpretation of the situation. Knowing what I know now about dissociation and his self-states, I'm pretty sure he was hearing a self-state saying that word about her and then seeing her lips move made it seem like it came from her. How do you navigate relationships when there appears to be such a disconnect? As I lacked other reasonable strategies, I chose to affirm both perspectives. I validated the big feelings each one was experiencing without adding judgment or taking a side. At the core, they did not trust each other because every memory held moments where one thrived and the other suffered. Their life pattern had taught them, "I am safe if someone else is in pain." If one child was crying and the second started crying because they were angry, the original child would stop crying. It had been so woven into their subconscious that someone else's "suffering" meant they didn't have to feel the physical or emotional pain.

Unintentionally parents perpetuate the cycle of distrust and competition by blame-finding and penalizing what is not the root issue. Uno is a perfect example. A child unable to keep their feet off the in-play Uno cards appears to need a consequence. "You don't get to play the game with us until you play kindly." Or the next time he asks to play, the kids say, "You don't play nice, and no one wants to play that with you." The child may learn to shift their behavior externally. However, their internal self is still festering in their wounds. Remember, the ANP manages daily functions and relationships. It can adapt, but the EP will continue to feel distrust and rejection. The more exhausting yet compassionate approach is to play Uno with the child one-on-one. Again and again, until they realize they are capable of playing the game with others. Then you weave them into playing with others while remaining present to navigate the hiccups along the way. Affirming this is a fun way to connect, not "Uno Hunger Games", where only one person comes out alive.

There are also times when trauma bonding can occur with acquaintances. An example is you and a classmate sitting in your seats waiting for the bell to ring. A student walks into the room, throws a chair, yells at the teacher, and then runs out. You both have observed a stressful and potentially dangerous interaction. Neither of you contributed to this situation, and neither of you is to blame. If the teacher messages the front office, shuts the door, and says, "Well, class, that was intense! Let's get on with the lesson." You may still have adrenaline running through your system, but you will feel a return to "normal". If the teacher starts crying or yelling at the class, "This is what's wrong with all you kids. There is no respect!" and starts handing out detention sheets to everyone in the class or saying, "Why didn't you stop him?" - the adult's shift in emotional responsibility to the students can cause a traumatic connection with another student. The students may try to protect each other, protect themself, or vilify the teacher because they internalized the teacher's stress as self-blame.

Some people also experience bizarre interactions from inner parts feeling "magnetized" to other people's internal parts. This can feel like living a different reality. It is like an inner part seeking co-regulation and validation from an external source. This may be worth considering if you have a child who always attracts certain people. They are not "choosing" the wrong type of friends; there is something within your child that those friends draw to as protection, support, or compassion. For myself, individuals will share their painful experiences with me. At first, this alarmed me. Then I realized that when we do not have answers for our inner parts, they will seek out connections for healing. As an adult, I learned to set boundaries around my inner child. This reduced the "beacon" attracting others. An example I have observed is when a child's inner self feels highly unsettled by another child's inner self, they may physically invade the other child's space. Child A experiences a heightened sense of being "on guard". Child B senses Child A's guardedness and their own sense of anxiety alerts. Child A then physically enters Child B's space - seemingly magnetized. It is a proactive dominant stance - that neither child may consciously acknowledge. When I recognize this interaction, I will have a child stand by me and prompt them to reflect on what their body is feeling. I give them an escape from the interaction and later discuss what we can do differently next time.

-You have your own story

Every child is also entitled to their own perspective. I use the "driving in a car" analogy. When I make a left turn while driving, I consider multiple factors (distance of oncoming traffic, light color, etc.). A child in the middle left side will not see any cars coming in our direction but will feel the car turning. The person in the front passenger seat will see the color of the light and the space between us and the other vehicles. The person in the back right seat may see a car approaching as we turn and think we will get hit. This child may have a higher anxiety level in the car than a child sitting in a different position. In any given family scenario- there will be multiple perspectives for what has occurred and why. It is vital to allow kids to ask questions about family choices and responses and give them space to process without diminishing their experience. I may have a very logical, adult reason, but that does not diminish the feelings they experience. When we use a dissociation lens, recognizing their self-state's experiences of being silenced, I want to give the kids all the information they need to reconcile their memory with reality.

Children who experienced trauma and dissociative shifts need validation that their perspective is accepted. Adults attempting to cover dangerous behaviors will tell a child, "You didn't experience what you think happened", or "It wasn't that big of a deal". Affirming a child's food preferences, imaginative stories, and emotional responses helps lay a foundation for "My perspective is valid". All kids need this. Kids with trauma histories will already have a shaky foundation of truth/perspective/opinion. The EP will "scream" out in whatever behaviors possible to get anyone to believe their experience. Kids with bottom-up processing will experience the rejection of their sensory and thought perspectives millions of times. It often stems from adults needing to understand the point of the interaction. When someone is sharing their trauma or pain, they are not asking you to sign an affidavit committing to the story's truthfulness. They are explaining the cavernous depths of their pain. When someone shares their sensory experience or a rabbit trail of thought, they are not asking you to repair their experience. They ask to be seen, known, and held safely in a space that can feel lonely.

All family members benefit from a home environment that respects the needs of each person. Children with internal parts can learn to nurture and care for each aspect of themself. Siblings will learn how to advocate for their own needs and to support the needs of others. Each family member can cultivate new pathways when they have connection with themself and others.

Resources

9

Going Forward

The risk of us ignoring dissociation is the perpetuation of intergenerational trauma, compounding childhood development delays, and pursuit of unhelpful treatments that worsen the symptoms. Generally speaking, it takes an individual six years or more to receive a Dissociative Disorder diagnosis. Complex-PTSD is still not fully recognized or confused with diagnoses like Borderline Personality Disorder. Though we know that rates of child abuse are high and abusive family environments perpetuate violence, children experiencing dissociation from PTSD are infrequently diagnosed. There are valid reasons to avoid diagnosing: risks of misdiagnosing too early, the stigma that follows a child through their life, insurance hiccups, and uncertainty of future child development. However, by waiting to address childhood dissociation, the dissociative episodes become more solidified within a child, who grows into an adult with structural dissociation.

Reactive Attachment Disorder (RAD) is associated with children who have experienced traumas and adoption. If you run in adoption circles, you may hear horror stories from parents, desperate pleas for rehoming, and lots of hopelessness. I believe that RAD actually describes a child with unstable inner parts. Children who experience traumas that impact their neural development so strongly they do not attach to themself. As their internal self-state rotates between younger and older, the child will not have memories or connections with their current home and parental units. The rules appear different, the support system seems different, and there is no consistent understanding of the environment or attachment to the self. The ANPs and EPs ride a roller coaster no one is driving. Caregivers focused on the child "attaching to the parent" detract from the child attaching to themselves. They need a trustworthy internal guide to facilitate a safe internal space for the inner child parts.

Starfish children did not choose to experience the harmful situations that caused their splits. They spend a lifetime carrying the burden of healing for traumas they did not choose. Often their habitats are inhospitable to growth - causing more splits and stunted growth to occur. Imagine a galaxy of severed armed starfish lying on the ocean floor. Would we work to change the pollutants, the temperature, find a better habitat? Or would we chastise the starfish for losing limbs? Blaming the creature for the failures of its environment does not produce health and vitality. Blaming the child for the failures of their environment or the family's intergenerational choices does not produce health and vitality.

The need to address dissociation in minor and major forms benefits the suffering child, the family, and the greater community. These individuals deserve to be seen in their humanity- receiving compassion and acceptance in every form. Providing safe spaces requires caregivers, practitioners, teachers, and support individuals must be aware of their internal selves. Many of these kids do not know the power they contain. Someone who does not know they are an energy sender or environment changer can cause havoc within a space. They can also provoke a lot of positive and good.

Visualization:

Take a moment and picture a time when you felt the air around you- alive with electricity. Maybe you were outside during a lightning storm or waiting for the headlining artist at a concert. You can feel the electrons, protons, and neutrons even though they are invisible. Sit for several minutes remembering how you felt - your physical sensations, emotions, thoughts. The thickness in the air. The stirring of your stomach, anticipating excitement. Prickles or goosebumps on your arm. Did you feel safe? Did you feel uncertain? Did you increase your observation of the environment? If picturing a concert, did you let yourself flow with the crowd's excitement or resist to maintain your composure? If picturing the lightning storm, did you feel awe, fear, or meh?

This energy surge can happen in positive ways. We were at my daughter's highly anticipated basketball game. The people in the stands were buzzing with excitement. The step team started their first stomp- to welcome the home team- and it was like a wave of energy hit the crowd. This sensation can also occur in negative situations. The tension rises until an inexplicable shift occurs, and a fight or yelling begins. Children with heightened sensory receptors and children with dissociated parts are incredibly attuned to "electrical shifts" within environments. These are the change makers. The environment shifters. The prophets. The artists. The singers. The inventors. The disruptors. These children are powerful treasures who deserve to be seen in their multi-faceted existence and given safe, compassionate environments to thrive.

10

Potential Indicators of Dissociation

Caregivers who seek out help for their children may feel like each behavior is a separate silo. A pediatrician will cover some bases, an Occupational Therapist will cover others, a teacher will see some of your child's behaviors, and the family may see another side. Caregivers may question if they actually see these indicators or if they reflect the caregiver's stress. If the only commonality with these symptoms is the child, often the child becomes "the problem". Some dissociative strategies reflect a specific diagnosis; others only require awareness and support. Some of these indicators can be indicative of more than one need. This is not a checklist, but it can provide you with language and understanding to better advocate for yourself and your children.

Remember that dissociation occurs on a spectrum. Just because your child daydreams does not mean they have a dissociated internal self. Some behaviors may indicate bottom-up thinking: which requires connective strategies for healthy development. Additionally, this book's focus is the development of dissociation for kids. These behaviors may look different in an adult compared to a child. If you are unsure or are a caregiver who may have experienced dissociative strategies, I have found it helpful to ask people around me, "What is your experience?", "Is this something you do?" or "What is considered 'normal'?" These questions benefit bottom-up thinkers who require a baseline to compare their situation against.

1. Time

Difficult time of year or time of day. Challenging situations may have occurred on or near these days, requiring dissociative strategies. For example, a child who experiences a violently angry drunk parent every Christmas may experience physical stressors surrounding that holiday. Or a child who has negative experiences with a parent may act out on Mother's or Father's Day, causing further disruption and stress. The child may not be "choosing" to do this but feels helpless with the flood of memories, sensations, and perceptions. A child integrated into a new home may experience deep longing at these times of the year. Depending on the response of the adoptive family, the child may receive support or feel pushed to disembody from their emotions. This can also be true of individuals with high sensory sensitivities- family gatherings may be unpredictable, loud, and stressful. As children, they learned to shut down during these gatherings.

Disruptions at the same time every day may be an indicator they are struggling to integrate some trauma or stress. I was flooded with anxiety and helplessness every day at 1:50- I stress-ate and was irritable in conversations. I finally connected that for several years- 1:50 was when I would pick up all five kids from school. The conversations, the snapping, the noise, and the stress had been too sensory-intense for my body. I was still holding on to the muscular tension and the fear of an impending meltdown, with little feeling of control and self-trust. This was not a response to a current situation but something else woven into my emotional and muscular memory.

Time confusion can look like a child asking, "Because it's a three-day weekend, does that mean we are off school for 21 days or 3 days?" This jumble of time concepts can indicate a confused internal state - if it is developmentally appropriate for the child to understand time concepts. Struggle with routine or predictability is common, but confusion surrounding the purpose of time can indicate inner confusion. If you always have dinner at 6:30, and the child is confused, "Am I in trouble? Why am I eating now?" - this could indicate a different ANP needing clarification.

2. Hoarding

Hoarding food is a common strategy to feel safe and retain control for a child. When children feel safe eating, without guilt about their urgent need, they learn to recognize the hunger sensation and other emotions that may trigger the "food" response. Children who integrate shame with their desire to eat or hoard will fall further into their cycle. Hoarding can be seen as the ANP needing food because it thinks it's taking care of the child. Years ago, I heard a loud noise at 3 in the morning. I went to the kitchen to discover my daughter standing with a handful of candy and candy spilled on the counter. "I was just cleaning up the jar." I stared at her, internally rolling my eyes, "Cleaning up the jar that you spilled?" At the time, I handled it by saying 'thank you' and helped her go back to bed with one piece of candy. I wonder if her younger self had gone to take the candy and her elder self "awoke" and was just as startled by her surroundings as I. Another child asked to keep an applesauce packet in her room - she had been waking up for a month, crying and afraid she would starve. The applesauce packet never got eaten but remains on her bedside table, so she knows she is safe. Viewing hoarding and food issues as an indicator of dissociation would help caregivers and clinicians recognize and "listen" to these parts, which may provide a longer-term cohesion than just providing safety and sustenance. The child can also develop self-trust and self-provision in a way that benefits all persons involved.

3. Lying

Lying is face-saving, protective, and elicits a sense of control. Lying is not always intentional. Yesterday, in response to a simple question, "Where are your shoes?" One child looked at me and rattled off a string of statements, "Yes, they are. I put them away. [they were obviously on the floor still]. I was wearing a different pair." Then her eyes widened, and she nervously laughed. She took a deep breath, slowed down, and accurately identified her shoes. For this child, lying is a stream-of-conscious approach to minimizing uncomfortable conversations. She is less likely to rattle off untruths when she pauses before answering. I am learning to give her space and internally catch up to honesty. We also learned to phrase questions or prompts to avoid "gotcha" questions. For example, asking, "Where are your shoes?" When they are obviously on the floor can feel accusatory. Asking or prompting, "Please put your shoes away." gives a direction without feeling like a trick. If you want them to discover what is out of place, you can prompt, "Scan the room and find 4 things that belong to you to put away."

Lying can be an internal part trying to protect or speak from their perspective. Last week I asked one child a question. He responded with a bold lie; midway through answering, I saw his self-state shift. He physically shook (like he was cold), laughed, and said, "That's not true!", then answered honestly. Getting to this place where lying isn't vilified and they can try again has taken a lot of work. The other self-state may not even know what was said or the fear the other part is experiencing. Before honesty can become a valued characteristic, the selves must trust each other, and there must be practice in recognizing how the self feels inside.

4. Academics

Poor academics can also be a signal of dissociation. It is vital to differentiate between a deficit because of early trauma, a learning disability, and what is from a different self-state or derealization. One of my kids frequently jumped around in her grades. An 'A' on a spelling test one week, followed by an 'F' the next. We wondered if there was a learning disability, ADHD, a low IQ, or trouble with comprehension - but there was no clear pattern. I realized that when we did many connective interventions, her anxiety decreased, and she aced her spelling test and absorbed other information. She was in her zone of proximal development. Sometimes she would switch to a mental space that didn't allow her to do any schoolwork. Any information taught would directly leave her thoughts. She would be super frustrated and unable to rebound. Any attempt at encouragement met stress signals: anxiety hands rubbing back and forth, tilting back and forth on her heels, and "unseeing" eyes. It was like handing a 2-year-old a stack of homework and then being surprised they were unable to complete it. She would be equally as shocked and internalize shame about it, which caused her to stall out further.

Identifying and simplifying the roots of a response can be incredibly challenging when there are so many layers of stressors presenting. "Is she going to have a full-scale meltdown? Do I need to put the other kids in a safe space? Can dinner wait while I help her to settle? Haven't we talked through this issue a thousand times? What brain bridge is collapsing right now? I feel so depleted. Why do we have to deal with this now?" Then practically, you must decide: does she just need someone to be present? Does she need to complete the schoolwork, or is it "non- essential"? Does she need comfort right now and a more in-depth check-in later? Is this her current age experiencing an internal struggle? Is this a younger self-state that needs compassion, acceptance, and equipping? Her stress highly reflects anxiety, and her moments of disconnect strongly reflect PTSD.

5. Transitions

For a child who consistently struggles with transitions, seems confused about standard rules in the transition place, or seems hypervigilant about transition times, it could indicate that they need an embodied strategy to help them with the transitions. It could indicate an ANP is struggling to transition. An extreme example occurred during our second playdate with our kids through DCS, very early in the transition process. When the social worker arrived to pick up the kids after our outing to a museum was over, one of the children collapsed to the floor, frozen. She could not move. It was not a "tantrum", as I had seen other kids have at transition times. No amount of coaxing or prompting received a response. Obviously, this was a stressful situation- meeting a new family, spending a day with strangers, over-stimulating, and not having a choice as a child. This freeze response at transitions happened for our first year together. It is essential to recognize when a child is not being defiant, but their system is overloaded.

6. Forgetful/memory loss

My daughter had asked me a question with a cheery attitude. I responded. 5 minutes later, she looked at me and asked the same question, this time with a grumpy expression. My other daughter looked at me, eyebrows raised. I said, "Sweetie, I just explained that to you". She looked up at me, "No you didn't, or I would have heard you." This scenario has played out repeatedly in my house over the past several years. Easily written off as a child being distracted or "It's the answer the kid didn't want." But the frequency with which it happens, generally with a shift in mood is interesting. Other times it will look like forgetting the location of items, or familiar places become unfamiliar. I have viewed this as a child needing to rehearse thousands of times to develop a pattern. If it is a different self-state, then it IS a new experience. It is a typical human experience to forget what they did at school or where they placed something. For a child who experiences dissociation, "memory loss" may be a separate part of them experiencing or remembering. Depending on the dissociative spectrum, it may be more like they were "watching a movie" about recess rather than fully being present at recess.

7. Motor control

Sudden stumbling or clumsiness can be an indicator of dissociation. There can be many reasons for an uptick in tripping or bumping into things. The child could be distracted, going through a growth spurt, doesn't have good spatial recognition, is trying to passive-aggressively express their displeasure at something, or express affection by bumping into you. The list could go on. However, when my daughter consistently walks into a room and steps on people's feet, it is always in conjunction with another indicator of dissociation. I just had to learn to look for it. Our response had been, "Please be mindful of the people near you". Now we recognize her age has shifted, and she needs different stimuli. Another example of motor control changing is clear handwriting becoming ineligible. A younger self-part may need developmental help with motor functions.

8. Bathroom or Food regression

There can be numerous reasons why a child may lose control of bodily functions. Sometimes they are simply too distracted. Other times it is an indicator of physical pain. Sometimes they are angry, and it is a control issue. Knowing your child, their development, and their trauma history - could this be a dissociated part needing help with bathroom skills? Similarly, with food: preference, appetite, or utensil usage may change. A child may test the system to see what they can get away with at the dinner table. Other times they may have a sensory response to certain foods. Preferences change. Other times a child may experiment with how they eat because it is fun or gets a good reaction from the parents. Knowing your child's preferences and sensory needs - is there a pattern of when they crave certain foods or how they handle eating? When these experiments or regressions occur with other indicators, exploring if a self-state needs developmental or communication support is helpful.

9. Ability to "override" meds

We had attempted several medicines with one child. We utilized the DNA test to ensure we found a medication that worked with his physiology. We did brain mapping, which gave insight into the neural structure and indicated "over-medicated" or "under-medicated". With heightened anxiety, he could not focus, even though his medicine treated attention and impulsivity. The medication would seem to work for a few weeks and then appear to lose efficacy. We would question if the dose needed to be more or if he needed a different mixture. It was ineffective even when he was on a medicine that should have helped him sleep better. Teachers would report that it seemed to work one day and not the next. When we realized that his self-states shifted, I could see how the medicine impacted some internal parts but not others. Bizarre but an indicator. "Healing the Fractured Child" by Frances S. Waters has a chapter dedicated to the pharmacological interactions of children with dissociation. This chapter is a great resource covering a variety of medications, indicators, and research.

10. Parent's Frustration

If a parent is consistently saying that "nothing seems to work", it may be that they do not have the skill set to manage their situation. It may also be that the child is shifting self-states, and the parent has been unable to get appropriate professional help. Often the parent's desperation is seen as needing extra training (which is valuable), or they need better self-care (which is also highly plausible). When a parent lives with the continual sense that "something is not right", it is valuable to push into an area they may not have considered. Realizing a child has differing self-states does not resolve the stress, but it does express a legitimate reason for the behaviors and responses. It affirms the parent has not lost their mind and that their perceptions were accurate. This paves the way for self-compassion, the ability to meet the self-states, and stabilization.

11. Defiance

Defiance and desperate disconnection are strategies to self-preserve and to keep others at arm's length. They may find cause and effect confusing, even though you have explained it a thousand times. New systems may seem tricky, even if you have already explained the directions several times. It is not a cognitive choice to disregard instructions but the self-state shifting that contributes to the uncertainty and "defiant" choices. If we view these behaviors as communication from inner parts trying to understand and respond to the world around them, then there is the potential to bring calm and alignment to them.

An inability to be held accountable can also be an indicator. A child who experiences depersonalization will feel a detachment from the experience. Cause and effect will appear "out of their control". A child who experiences derealization may feel victim to the environment or circumstances around them - again having a low locus of control. A child with dissociative parts or internal confusion may not accept responsibility because it was not their fronting part who did the action.

12. Attachment

A constantly switching self-state will look like it has varying attachment styles. It is sometimes connected, other times ambivalent, and other times confused. When the caregiver attempts to interact the way they did the day before or even 5 minutes ago, the self-state will respond with confusion and rejection. Imagine you "woke up" and found car keys in your hand and a loan document under your pillow. You would push back and say, "Where did this come from? I didn't sign up for this! Who put me up to this?" It would feed paranoia, self-preservation, and resistance against those trying to convince you otherwise. A child who has bonded with a caregiver while in one self-state may feel appalled and duped in another. Recognizing differing self-states helps caregivers to learn to bond with each differing self-state instead of presuming acceptance.

13. Overly responsible (Fawn Response)

At times a child may take on the persona of a grown-up. Taking care of others, dictating rules, hovering in spaces. For some children, this is just the role they had growing up, and it is natural for them to feel responsible for caring for others. The sudden pretentious leadership role can feel confusing for a child who is routinely forgetful and impulsive. Sometimes it can feel like the child is manipulating situations or trying to show off when others are having a hard time. Once we realized that some self-states take on the persona of an adult, it made much more sense. They weren't trying to micromanage everyone. They just felt unsteady, and the adult persona decided to handle everything. This might come as a relief, "Phew! Finally, X is remembering where things belong and remembering the rules!" But, if it is an internal part functioning responsibly, our encouragement of those choices may actually encourage the EP to take over and not respect the age of the child's body.

14. Freeze response

When a child is in freeze mode, it comes from their highly dysregulated nervous system. It can look like depression, lethargy, and dissociation (derealization, depersonalization). This could indicate an inner ANP that needs help returning to baseline. Freeze can also look like non-compliance. Just the other day, one of my kids spilled water on the table. They moseyed to get a towel. The spill was near my computer, and I yelled, "Hustle!" The child froze. I yelled again. The child could not move. I felt irritated and grabbed a towel. After a few minutes, the child said, "Mom, I can't move when I'm yelled at. I shut down." I know this, yet my urgency overrode what would have been more effective.

15. Flight/Fight

Survival brain responses are intended for when a child is in survival mode. If this is the constant level a child is functioning from - we need to consider the role of dissociation. Shifting our interactions from the higher brain to the lower brain helps to de-escalate. This can help a child calm down to process a situation. One of my kids has come home multiple days this week having uncharacteristically picked fights at school. As I processed what she may be experiencing, I remembered a younger self-state was fairly aggressive and maybe was still holding on to frustration that she was trying to release. Sometimes these responses indicate a lower brain response, and other times a shift into a different self-state. If a different self-state has switched, it indicates that the current self was so overwhelmed that a different one needed to take over.

Learning to track triggers for the current self can help calm the self-state and help them to avoid switching in moments of stress.

16. Multiple Doctors

If the family or child has visited multiple doctors or therapists and received little feedback or improvement in overall functioning, it is worth checking out the child's tendency to dissociate. Seeing a doctor several times and describing the symptoms will not always lead to the correct diagnosis. Depending on how the child functions during the visit, their apparent needs may or may not be revealed. Depending on which self-state is presenting, the needs can shift.

17. Pain

Pain that does not have a clear origin can be another indicator. Some kids have lots of owies as a form of connection to an adult's empathy. A child who experienced traumas at a young age may have an EP that frequently shows their owies to the adult. Picture a 2-year-old needing a band- aid, but the child is a 14-year-old. Other kids have lots of owies because they play intensely. Some kids have stomach pains because of anxiety; the ANP could experience nausea on behalf of the child. Another child has leg pain that has been tested, dismissed, and given stretches - yet it remains. We are in the beginning stages of piecing together the origins of the self-state that know and hold on to that pain. Another child will exclaim, "This finger feels this way!" In a new-to-them way, but will have already told us about it. It is like they are a baby staring at fingers they didn't know belonged to them. Sometimes it is a challenge to determine a "pain scale" due to depersonalization.

18. Objects/Stealing

Random objects in a backpack or room can look like a child is stealing and lying. Sometimes that is the case. Sometimes they trade toys or jewelry. Sometimes kids buy friendships with items. Sometimes, someone will grab something and have zero memory of it. Depending on the self-state, this could be something that it feels is needed for survival, worth, or protection. Assuming a child enjoys disrespecting property is a heavy burden for a kid to carry. When we can look into other self-states and remove the pressure of shame-filled consequences, a child feels freer to learn a new identity, acquire new behaviors, and feel safe when they err.

19. Imaginary Friends

Kids are wired to have an imagination that explores and helps them to make sense of the world around them. Some kids will have a stuffed animal that is a playmate, other children may have invisible friends, and others may have none. Imaginary friends do not determine "dissociation"; however, when a child has experienced trauma and has imaginary friends, it is worth exploring to see if they are self-states. Even referring to other parts of their brain can indicate a fractured self. One time I told my child, "It seems like I say something, and there's a little man in your ear who listens and decides if you need the information." He looked at me, nodding, "Well, he guards the gate so not everything can get in." I thought he was merely going on with my scenario at the time. Later it made more sense from the self-state perspective. These imaginary friends could also be imaginary enemies - if a child feels "haunted", there could be a part that needs safety.

20. Reflexes

If a mismatched or reduced reflex occurs, it could also indicate a different self-state that is functioning. The Moro or startle reflex typically goes away after four months. If a child continues to exhibit this high startle reflex, it can influence the dissociation they experience. Allowing that self-state to grow in its reflexes will enable the entire person to function more fluidly. Reduced or no reflex can indicate high dissociative tendencies in a child. For example, when one of my children is in a detached (derealization) state, they will not notice or flinch if anything dangerous is near them. After several "near-miss" instances, we quickly recognize any potential hazards when she cannot notice them for herself.

21. Restless/High Energy

I have noticed a correlation between my son's times with overwhelming energy and his shift in self-states. Some self-states are more lethargic, so this is not an "across-the-board" label. If it seems that their energy or inability to focus fluctuates, then explore if there is a trigger or age self-state that shifts during certain moments of the school day or certain times at home. When a self-state is frantically trying to find a way to ground itself, the usual approaches of exercise or movement breaks may block its ability to focus. Providing activities to hone in their focus, like sketching or tracing, help the mind to settle back into the right level of self-hierarchy. We use the example of herding kittens to discuss "collecting our thoughts". If I chased the kittens, I might eventually find them all after running and scattering them first (movement, energy exertion). If I sit with treats and calmly allow the kittens to come to me, I achieve the goal with less exertion and a sense of urgency (grounding, calming). For these outliers, energy-release activities often prompt an adrenaline surge instead of a settling connection.

22. Sexual Activity

-Sexual interactions should involve consent - not just verbal "yes", but also bodily consent (muscles relaxing, openness). Ongoing pain, headaches, and inability to locate where sensations occur can be indicators of dissociative sexual encounters. Using alcohol or other substances to mask discomfort can lead to numbing long-term. A glass of wine or edible to relax differs from "fueling in order to function". For individuals who have a history of trauma, there is a risk of further harming ANPs or EPs with activities they do not consent to.

-Constant pursuit of sexual stimulation can be an indicator of a different internal part. An internal part could be trying to "reconcile" a previous experience, needing an energy release, or needing the 'shutdown' if their body numbs out. A younger part may equate this with comfort instead of a sexual experience. There may be an ANP that feels powerful initiating and guiding a sexual encounter.

23. Dangerous

A perplexing side of dissociative states is the extreme way some of them communicate. Fires, self-harm, hurting others, and hurting animals can all be indicators that something is going on with a different self-state. It could also be a lack of awareness of personal safety. When going to a new place, one of my children will find precarious ledges to walk on. Another child will intentionally stand near a volatile or unpredictable person. Other times a child will start mindlessly grinding something into their skin, "unaware". These moments are frightening yet communicate a desperate need for help and calm. Recognizing them as self-states that need to be heard instead of "anger problems" or "lack of self-worth" will go far in helping the states to feel safe and able to express their pain.

24. Intellectualization

Avoiding feelings by researching, avidly talking, and acquiring more information can be a form of disconnect from the body. As a parent, I acquired as much information as possible to avoid feeling the grief and helplessness I was experiencing. My brain naturally gathers information and seeks patterns. I learned my teachers wanted to hear information exchanged more than they wanted to hear about me having a hard time with friends at recess. I knew feeling emotions like love was hard, so I could exchange information on topics to show I cared. My therapists say I have a good grasp on what I am dealing with - but they miss that it is hard for me to feel what I am dealing with. A child who demonstrates this will need some assistance to counter-balance their left brain's heavy processing. Often the experience of "feeling" can be so vast they need a safe person to hold space for them to feel.

25. Daydreaming or being watched

Some kids think they are being watched and will "perform" for the pretend audience. This may be a way to practice social skills or avoid actual interactions. The child then feels supported without having the support of actual humans. Daydreaming can serve a similar function - it envisions our desires in a way the child doesn't know how to express other- wise. Imagination and pretending are developmentally appropriate for children. A child that can not bridge between pretend and a tangible world is experiencing dissociation from their environment.

26. Sensory Shifts

One of my kids experiences a shift in temperature when they are slowly dysregulating. They always get cold before their mind shifts. Now we recognize the "cold" prompt as a chance to get the appropriate stimulation input or take a break. Some people will experience a difference in sight when a dissociative shift occurs. Sound, taste, touch, balance, and inner awareness all can be impacted by a different ANP or a milder form of dissociation.

11

Connective Strategies

This chapter will outline practical strategies and activities based on the 4-C framework (curiosity, compassion, connection, cultivation). If the child and adult are within their zone of regulation and have the capacity for curiosity and connection, they can work on further cultivating activities. If a child or adult is not at baseline, then a cultivating activity should not occur. We should use a "return to baseline" approach. Recognize the capacity of yourself and your child. I suggest picking one or two strategies to integrate initially. Even as adults, we have neural pathways well paved in old habits. As we acquire new tools and methods, our brains need time to practice and process these new strategies. Sometimes we learn better while working alongside another adult who can model healthy responses. In a stressed environment, an entire overhaul at once will lead to exhaustion, not long-term change. This chapter has activities for returning to baseline, curiosity, connection, cultivation, dissociation focus, and self-correcting questions. Compassion is the thread that weaves safe relationships together.

Baseline:

-*Music/Beats/Patterns*- Rhythm is regulating. Humming a tune, tapping out a beat, and the sound of footsteps are all options for getting a child to baseline. If a child needs co-regulation by holding hands and swaying, be intentional about matching their pace and then slowing down bit by bit. When the game "My Singing Monsters" was popular, I would start singing or humming one part and have my child add another sound. Integrating with another person allows the brain to begin to seek connective feedback. For a dissociative child, co-regulation may not be an option initially. A focused activity (connect the dots, picture find book) or a video with low stimulation and clear order can function like a calming pattern. Hand buzzers (therabuzzers) are handheld devices that send out a small electrical current. These are non-invasive and can supplement other strategies.

-Below Baseline- When a highly dysregulated child cannot follow direct instructions, it can look and feel aggressive/disruptive. I will try to find a "below baseline" skill they are getting right. For example, one time, a student was pacing a classroom. They were bumping into cabinets and refusing to sit. I felt myself feeling flooded and knew the class was feeling the same way. I ignored them for a bit, then acknowledged the child and said, "Thank you for walking in a way that gave space to your classmates." A bit later, the child sat down and did their work. You know as well as I do that these are "flip-a-coin" situations. Every time it lands on "heads," the child will comply, and every time it lands on "tails", the child will refuse. From a dissociation standpoint, children with attention-seeking behavior have an inner state needing attention. The child may not be able to provide that inner self with structure. Situations can be diffused if an external adult can recognize the internal self's ability to do a "below development" skill.

-Give Space- Sometimes kids and adults just need space to feel bad. A dysregulated child can not process immediate instructions. A child whose exhaustion or hunger triggers a dissociative shift will need space to re-recognize their environment. The primary way we give space is by reducing our demands until after the need is satisfied. We will also help the environment to shift. One of my kids felt sad and wanted to cry. No tears would come out. She could not move past this sadness. I asked if

turning on sad "break-up" music was alright. She nodded. Everyone in the room cried to the sadness, and then we moved on.

-*Herding Kittens*- When a child's energy is off-the-charts, or their choices are highly impulsive and frantic: Energy is not always a signal of needing physical exertion. Sometimes boundless energy is the brain and body over-functioning and feeling out of control. It is like "herding kittens" - the child has one thought, then the next comes running through, and on and on. We approach this boundless energy by doing a focused activity like picture find, dot-by-dot picture, sketching, or a fine motor activity. Honing their mental focus allows us to address the boundless energy and find a directed activity. Another strategy is to list off all the thoughts in their mind; we affirm how much information their mind holds! If the child does not want to do an "activity"- I ask them to make a list of groceries, write down the names of family members for holiday gifts, sort out drying markers, or sharpen colored pencils. These tethering activities pull the neural responses back into a contained path.

Curiosity:
-*Join in with a behavior of your child.*
Goal: Gain insight into the experience of the child. Parallel play is an invitation to connection. Copy their behavior (humming, spinning, tapping a pencil, throwing a pillow, etc.).

Slow down and speed up your movements, or change the intensity levels. Reflect on what you are experiencing - what sensations or emotions do you feel? If you are doing this with a child, you can ask them to correct or model for you the right way to do this. If the child is non-verbal or low-verbal, follow their actions and observe if they begin to modify, following their cues. If the behavior is a non-safe behavior, as the adult, take time on your own to visualize what may occur within that scenario. Use your experiences and visualizations to ask your child questions. For example, one child craved forceful movements and felt "oppositional". I gave them markers to make dots with, force-fully destroying the marker tip. A traditional "don't do that" behavior encouraged an energy release and exploration of our feelings.

-Shift physical space or role reversal.

Goal: Changing the physical dynamic can give us insights we over-look.

Adults can kneel on the ground or lower themself and look from the child's view. Have the child stand on a chair and give instructions. If a child dislikes their room, sit in it as they turn off the lights and shut the door- what feelings or sensations do you experience? Put the child in charge of getting everyone out of the house for an outing. Be curious about how they express urgency or instructions. How does it feel to be rushed or told what to do? If your kids have a stressful go-to game (tag, tetherball, clue, etc.), join in and let them give you instructions. These curious role reversals can provide invaluable insight.

-Retry:

Goal: Under stress, we often make poor choices. Retrying allows the child to stop, think, and show what they can do to their best ability. Their retry determines what I teach or how I respond. Notice which portion of the process they are unsteady in (can they identify the issue but not problem solve? Or can they come up with ideas but not identify the issue?)

A teenager comes home from school amped up from an argument with a friend, but they weren't kind in their words either. After vent-ing, I may ask, "How would you respond if you could do that over?" They have space to assess that relationship and determine their social risk and values. We will address, "If I knew to expect it, I would plan to fight them", differently than, "Next time, I would ask them what they were actually upset about and give them space." Another example is asking a child to put away their shoes and they throw them up the stairs. If I choose to get angry about their disrespect, the child may focus on their attitude or be defensive. If I say, "You have a chance to re-try and respectfully put your shoes away." The child gets to work on wiring the neural and muscle memory of putting the shoes away in a less disruptive way.

If the question arises, "But life doesn't give you second chances, what are we teaching them?" Or "Some choices can never be undone!" Reflect on your response and goal: Why am I jumping to a worst-case scenario? Did I have additional chances from my parents? Or my boss? How would it be different if I had second chances? Children who feel safe trying again, and recognize their caregivers as supportive, will be more likely to ask for help in those "too big to redo" scenarios. Children who are terrified of making mistakes will not ask for help. Children shamed for "doing it wrong" will not ask for help when they've dug holes too deep to climb out of. What is your goal?

-What were you hoping to feel? Is there a time when you felt that way?

Goal: Prompt the child to think of the motivation underneath a behavior. Stepping back from blame, we focus on the desired feeling and nurture the embodiment of the desired feeling. Try to remain curious with the child instead of directive.

NARM (Neuro Affective Relational Methods) encourages embodiment within the present moment. For example, one of my children had come home from school after witnessing a fight and a teacher getting knocked down by a student. He spent the afternoon at home picking verbal fights with the other children. Finally, he pushed someone down hard during a game of basketball. Our traditional approach with this child is to ask, "What is the action you did?", "Can you identify why you did it?", "What should you do differently?". His dissociative strategies taught him to disconnect from ownership of the situation- he could name his role, reason, and different approach- but from a derealization perspective, he felt it was a movie he was not really a part of.

Within this situation, I asked him, "What were you hoping to feel?" The child thought for a moment and said, "I wanted to feel powerful." I affirmed, "Powerful is a good feeling to have! Did you feel powerful at that moment?" He said, "Yes. Until they fell and then I didn't feel powerful, I felt scared." Again, I affirmed this insight. [The goal is to draw compassionate attention to what is taking place within his body and mind. He is learning to speak for himself, to advocate for a need, and to see that others respect his perspective. He is also learning that feeling "powerful" is not something to be ashamed of. Responding with compassion and curiosity gives space for the child to decrease their adrenaline and arousal. Once they return to a baseline, they can recognize that they remain connected and not alienated.].

Then I asked, "Is there a time when you did feel that powerful?" [This is to encourage internal resourcing. When they can access that memory and feeling, it creates a neural pathway that will continue to develop. Some children will be unable to think of a time when they had independence, consent, or power - you can ask about a movie or book where they have seen that and then how they felt inside watching it.] My son couldn't think of a time when he felt particularly powerful. I asked, "I wonder if you felt something similar when we were at the amusement park, and you went on that big ride alone?" He thought about it and then named, "Yeah, I liked feeling like I could see everyone and no one could get me!" His power seemed connected to safety and feeling larger than others. You could comment on that or mentally note that theme for future interactions. We also named that sometimes an action does not feel powerful at the moment but only afterward.

-How do you wish this happened?

I often use this question when a child is in a "stuck" scenario (an unresolvable situation with a sibling, denying an obvious wrong choice). It also is used when a child refuses to complete a task or has a "lazy access" reflex. (Lazy access is my term for someone expecting the other person to do the mental work for them.) Often when the kids have the chance to share their underlying resistance, they can shift and complete the task or resolve an issue. For example, if two kids argue over clothes - I will say, "Let's pause the issue of this specific shirt. How do each of you wish this scenario played out differently?" The child who was aggressive can restate their desire, and the child who felt attacked can defend themself. We then clarify the house expectations and, if necessary, have the kids redo the interaction. Letting kids untangle their own stories in a compassionate environment allows them to build trust with themselves and the caregiver. A few nights ago, a child approached me at bedtime after four years of using these strategies. They took a deep breath and said, "Mom, I am going to be honest. I have two pieces of gum hidden in my pocket." I would never have known, but they knew a house rule is not to have food or gum in bedrooms. I thanked him for his honesty and let him pick a safe spot in the kitchen to save the gum for the morning. Every time you and your child process "How I wish this had happened," it lays a foundation for a future choice. And as a bonus, the child knows they can trust themself to make a wise choice!

-Do you need a retry?

Goal: Giving the child a chance to retry allows them to demonstrate their ability and reinforces the neural development of a skill.

Kids who respond with attitude or refuse to do a task do not need their tension met with more tension. When they try to displace their aggression onto you, and you keep it- this dissociative strategy relieves them of responsibility. Allow the responsibility to remain on their shoulders while you maintain a compassionate and stable response. Giving a retry helps children develop their ability to access their mental "file folders". I am vested in building long-term strategies that impact their future academics, social life, and adult years. If a child asks a question I have already provided an answer to, I prompt them to use their resources. Pause and listen to their brain, check a calendar, google the answer, or ask a sibling. Generally, they discover the information.

Retries are helpful with attitude and tone of voice- we do not always hear how we sound. A gentle prompt, "You sounded kinda rude. Can you retry?" redirects the parent from feeling offended and encourages the child to self-check. Rushing through a chore and leaving it unfinished can be given a retry. I give my children equivalent homework if they fail a test they cannot retake. My concern is their ability to understand the work and build muscle memory.

Connection:
-Mirroring and Body Doubling
Goal: Encourage connection through copying or simultaneous activities. These can benefit younger internal parts who want to connect through play.

Mirroring activities include handclap games, copying facial expressions, following the leader, etc. Children who are able to make eye contact may enjoy a staring contest. You could plan a meal where one person "leads", and everyone has to mimic their eating speed and style. With one child, I found that hand clap games gave her predictable physical touch, eye contact, and the chance to mirror me. Eye contact and bonding are important developmental opportunities with her inner self, as we know much of her trauma happened in infancy.

Body doubling is similar to parallel play. If your child struggles with homework, having a warm body near them can help. Simultaneously doing chores, brushing teeth, and stretching are all opportunities to body double. Modeling an action is sometimes more impactful than a verbal prompt for neurodivergent children. Inner self-parts benefit from watching a suggested behavior modeled. If the child veers from expectation, prompt them to observe and adjust.

-Timeline
Goal: Create a tangible way to see each person in the family's history.
We used a long roll of butcher paper. We wrote our birth years and birth cities, starting with Joe and myself, then wrote significant dates

and places. Then we added a line for each child from their birth. We labeled where, when, who they lived with, and any significant events. The rolled paper is easy to pull out whenever a kid wants to look at it. I think it helps the dissociated parts see that we all existed before they knew us. It also helps kids think of questions they want to ask about specific times and places.

-Role Play

Goal: Practice interactions to gain relationship skills and to experiment "incorrectly".

We have a bowl in the middle of the dining table where the kids can put questions and topics for us to discuss at dinner. These topics vary from "farts" to friendship to the random sex question. We allow any discussion topic. It is sometimes awkward but always interesting! If a child struggles with a teacher, we let them practice appropriate and inappropriate responses. We practice responses to someone teasing so they can have a good phrase ready without coming up with one on the spot. They can also work through their negative feelings beforehand. We do not encourage yelling at authority figures; however, it is safe to get the anger off your chest in a role play. We practice how to "play the game" if you do not agree with the system or rules. Role-playing allows them to remain present within a moment, not needing to dissociate. They can think through possible repercussions and make a choice. A child gains confidence when they can make predictions and have known factors in advance of a situation. In situations where there may be zero-knowledge beforehand, we practice the choices we DO control. Role-playing allows neural development to occur in a neutral environ- ment.

One child was angry after school. They had a negative interaction with a staff member who did not know them. After venting and processing some, I had us practice "playing the game". For the next 10 minutes, the child had to do everything I said immediately. He was allowed to be angry but had to comply. I explained that I would rather he process his anger at home and be extra obedient with a new teacher. My final order was to stand with his nose on the front door. No one loves this feeling. The child was furious. After several minutes I said, "Right now, you are thinking all kinds of awful things about me, and that is ok. But I want you to think 'she is not making me be here. I am choosing to stand here!" Switch from being forced to choosing. He smiled - he got the point of the game. He can choose to comply not as submission but as a willful part in the "game". Kids with significant behaviors and potentially disruptive inner parts must practice these tricky situations in a safe environment.

Cultivation:

Cultivation is acquiring longer-term knowledge and strategies to thrive. This will involve teaching our children vocabulary and strategies to self-manage and thrive in the future.

-Senses Vocabulary-

When our kids are young, we teach them a basic knowledge of colors, numbers, senses, and body parts. We scaffold their learning as they age by introducing complex colors, letters used in place of numbers, and developing a robust vocabulary. We should also expand our explanation of senses. Giving kids this language allows them to recognize how they experience and respond to their environments. If a child says, "I don't like this food", I encourage them to identify why - taste, texture, length to chew, memory, etc. It is ok to have food preferences! It is ok to explain, "I can't eat X food because I gag when that texture is on my tongue." Equipping them with an expanded vocabulary lets them realize, "There isn't something wrong with me! I embody my experience in this world!"

Equipping kids with vocabulary and the ability to describe is essential for communicating their experiences. Sight, touch, smell, taste, and sound are the five senses we are most familiar with. There are three additional senses: Vestibular- a sense of balance and spatial orientation; Proprioception- awareness of the body in space and the amount of strength needed to do a task; and Interoception- awareness of internal bodily states. Individuals with ADHD, ASD, PTSD, and other forms of neural organization may experience some sensations more intensely than others. An individual who is blind or has a vision impairment will have stronger senses that guide them in their environment. Their proprioception and hearing may be more heightened. Similarly, a person with weak proprioception may use their sense of touch to determine their placement within a space. Constantly bumping into other people- unintentionally, yet without that "bump", they look lost and without roots. They are unaware of their placement in their environment.

The 6, 7, and 8th senses are important to teach because many individuals who dissociate do so based on their experience of the space around them. When we are unable to articulate our discomfort or the pressure we feel, everyone around us may act like that environment is normal. We choose to conform or meltdown - feeling we are the problem. If a child can recognize, "In this environment, I am feeling the pressure of certain adults." Or "I feel an icky stomach when this person talks", or "I don't have the right pressure to complete this task", or "People keep bumping into me, maybe I need a better zone of space"- they will remain connected their body and learn strategies to communicate to the world around them.

Ways to incorporate the expanded senses:

-As an adult, reflect on your own experience. What are your personal food preferences? Specifically, think about why you prefer or repel certain foods. How do you recognize space in the environment around you? Do you recoil from others, float around, or bumper cars with people or objects like tables or chairs? If you have difficulty recognizing your action - slow down and try to do an uncharacteristic action for yourself. For example, I don't bump into people - I give individuals a wide berth. When trying to understand myself better, I experimented with letting myself bump into objects or the people in my house (not aggressively!). I realized I experienced a fear of other people's responses. I had a little voice in my head reprimanding me, "Be mindful of your space". I had learned to find my place in a room by avoiding others and fearing being corrected. I don't want to bump into people - not to avoid a confrontation, but to feel rooted in an environment because I belong and know my area. These adult reflections will impact how we teach and guide our kids.

-For kids- begin to integrate the vocabulary into daily experiences. Affirm their awareness of themself. Children with heightened Interoception may feel their body coming down with a cold a few days before the virus fully hits. Suggest some strategies they can use to help (drink more water, take vitamin C, etc.), but affirm how great it is that they can "read" their body! I was annoyed when my kids had a new ailment to discuss at bedtime. My first thought is, "Are they stalling going to bed?" Now, I try to view it as their body tries to settle down from the day, they are naturally doing a body-scan. Sometimes that means moving bedtime earlier to accommodate the extensive body scan or having them journal. Body positivity and self-trust begin in these little ways. Instead of seeing our body as a problem, or we can't trust our interpretation of our own body - we recognize that our body is good and our brain validates what I am experiencing.

-**Sensory input**- Ongoing sensory input allows the brain to absorb information and integrates undeveloped pathways. The "art therapies continuum" is a resource that connects art mediums and children's emotional/mental functioning. If a child prefers pencil drawings, no-mess activities, and following the model drawing, it could show a heightened need for control and structure. You can find safe ways to help them experience messes, less control, and help them experience some messy emotions. If a child prefers large finger paints, huge movements, and is always outside the lines - you can find a safe way to help them "boundary" their experiences in a tangible way. Keeping this information in the back of your mind can guide what activities you give to each child. If I provide paint to my more "out-of-control" child, that paint will end up everywhere, even with the constant reminders to keep the paint within its space. Providing them a less messy option helps them build capacity for a more "controlled" tool. A child who always follows the example and colors within the lines may also receive more positive feedback. Unintentionally, the positive adult feedback may reinforce the child's internal anxiety - teaching them to avoid mistakes and that they are preferred when not messy.

The child's internal state may interact differently with similar mediums like slime, oobleck, play dough, or cloud foam. Adding vocabulary to these sensory experiences is important. "I don't like this" can be expanded to specifying texture, scent, density, or tingling in the belly. At home, we respect the developmental cycles our kids go through with various art forms. Sometimes they are in a fine-motor skill, controlled phase, and other times a messier, experiential phase. One way I include sensory experiences is during "listening" times. At home, when we read as a family - they can draw, do slime, fold origami, or make bracelets. Considering that many of these motor and sensory skills are acquired asynchronously by the neurodivergent population, reintroducing "early life" sensory items helps strengthen neural connections. Children with dissociated inner parts need sensory experiences they may have missed.

-Bottom-up thinkers begin with a sensory observation. Using sensory prompts can encourage participation. If you have a child who struggles to write or do an assignment- they do not necessarily need a movement break. They may need a connection between their fingers and their brain. Some options to encourage brain-finger connections include hand wiggling or tapping exercises or rubbing the hand with a textured surface.

-Bilateral stimulation and Opposites

Crossbody activities help keep the neural pathways activated by running criss-cross through the brain. This can be as simple as having the right arm touch the left knee and vice versa, or it can include learn- ing a new dance. Integrating cross-body movements as brain breaks in school or as media breaks at home is an easy way to reinvigorate the brain.

Sometimes we will have a goofy "crawl to your next station" or "bear crawl" for 5 minutes- these movements hit on an early life developmental skill and impact both sides of the brain working at once.

Do the opposite. Have the child do an unwanted behavior backward and then do the appropriate behavior. There was a child in a class I taught who would instantly do the behavior I told them not to do. "Do not jump and touch the projector chord." This child would already have jumped before I finished the sentence. It aggravated me and set a bad example to the class, but there was no "frontal lobe" thought process - it was all reaction. I began to have this child visually show the class what not to do and then what to do. In order to redirect his neural response, this child needed the physical acting out of the verbal statement. He could lead by example and help rewire his impulsive reaction. Pulling your hand away from an object (doing the behavior backward) and then doing the appropriate action can be done to a rhythm, acted out as a group, or reinforced when completed.

Do it backward. Writing with the opposite hand, walking backward, and brushing teeth in the opposite circle are all opportunities to reinforce neural pathways while normalizing "it's ok to feel wobbly when doing something new." Retracing our steps helps strengthen executive functions like "recall". If your child cannot find their shoes/ pencil/toy - prompt them to retrace their steps as if they were being rewinded. Walk backward, scan the room ceiling to floor - mixing up our approach will often expand our viewpoint- and they can find their missing object. Some experiments can occur that will be unsuccessful in a "backward" way. (Can I eat soup with an upside-down spoon? Can I oppositely tie my shoes?) If the goal is "to try it backward, " it is not a failure, just a judgment-free experiment. This safety in exploring establishes the "felt safety" necessary for the brain to process challenging situations.

-Describing and Imagination. Asynchronous development and gaps from trauma can impact the development of imagination and description. The brain stores early childhood memories in sensory,

pre-verbal portions of the brain, holding on to sensations and memories without having a language expression of them. Positive memories and traumatic experiences can be inaccessible via language but accessible via sensation. A certain smell or sound can throw a child back to a specific time and place. Some children are imaginative during stressful moments and can vividly describe details- but cannot describe daily, non-stressful experiences. These non-judgemental activities provide safe ways to expand imagination and description. Everyone has the right to experience the world in their unique way. Over time, these little activities allow inner parts of the self to feel safe and non-judged, which paves the way for greater connection.

Integrating description activities in their daily life can expand the vocabulary and the neural pathways between the left and right brain. Place an object in the middle of a table and see how many descriptions they can come up with, including as many senses as possible.

"Would you rather" games are good for asserting an opinion and justifying your reasons. For a kid who struggles with verbal expression, they could draw or show with props. "Snake Oil" is a fun description card game.

Music Draw is a fun activity to see how certain sounds feel. Play several songs from various styles of music. Provide different drawing supplies and prompt, "Draw however the music feels to you." You draw while the music plays. Afterward, they can explain the colors chosen, the shapes or lines, and how they felt while drawing.

Imagination is vital for learning and surviving. A child with an ANP (the internal part that handles daily functions) exists in their internal safety world while still needing to navigate the actual world. They need a bridge that connects their created world to the real one. A safe adult, imagining alongside the child, can affirm that their brain is a beautiful, fascinating place. We want to validate that these protective and creative measures are good and serve a purpose! A child frequently told, "Get your head out of the clouds", would benefit from an adult joining their universe to see what exists. A child still within their unsafe environment should not be forced out of their internal world until their external world can provide a matching safety. Disconnected imagination resides in the head, disconnected from the body. Bridging the imagination through drawing, words, dance, or creating can help the imagination become embodied. A child with a healthy and secure childhood will imagine while maintaining a connection to the world around them. There is a tethered or boundaried way in which they exist and create. The untethered, unboundaried imagination signifies disconnection from self and the environment. For example, one of my kids would tell fantastical tales of interacting with animals. On one family hike, they said squirrels threw acorns at them, and they had scratches from the acorns. Factually, the story was not accurate. Fictionally, it sounded like fun. Adults sometimes silence an imaginative story, "You know that isn't true!" Or "You know they weren't aiming right for you!". But what is the harm of connecting with the story? Is the child trying to feel brave while hiking? Or feeling a connection with nature? What if the child develops a real fear of squirrels after this experience - or refuses to go hiking again? I may explore pretend-play options that practice protecting oneself from a squirrel, looking for stories of bravery, using a hiking "helmet"- or other ideas to join in creatively. As we parent our children with openness and imagination, we experience a re-parenting of our own inner children. These inner children needed to explore, create and use imagination to process our life experiences.

-Nature

We have found that exploring and learning about the world helps our kids process life without a shame lens. Children who have been victims of unpredictable adult choices may experience reassurance in the patterns of nature. For a child who struggles with time orientation, looking past a clock, seeing the sun, and knowing that today is different than yesterday is valuable. Seeing the placement of the sun or a shadow and recognizing morning or afternoon is empowering. For kids who have unpredictable connections between cause and effect- it is an act of preservation to view one's self as the center of the universe in a squelching way. This "center of the universe" mindset can cause paranoia, anxiety, and existential stressors. For example, when you were younger, did you ever look out at the rain while feeling sad and think you caused the clouds to rain? For some kids who carry the weight of the world due to life's circumstances, it is a small imaginative leap to controlling nature. Learning about clouds and how rain forms takes a feeling, "Whenever I cry, it rains, therefore I made the rainfall," to "Coincidences happen between me and nature, that is cool," or "Sometimes when it rains, I feel melancholy."

We emphasize the theme that everything and everyone goes through change processes over time by discussing animal life cycles and erosion. Discussing nature bypasses shame by neutrally developing concepts around change, growth, and resiliency. Talking about seasons changing and hibernation provides a discussion on taking a break or the dormant cycle before plants burst into life. For my literal child, using facts of nature instead of nebulous emotions helps him to understand and change behaviors. Referencing a magnetic pull makes more sense than explaining a social cue. Showing a tomato caterpillar covered in wasp larva exemplify when other ideas or words take root in you and drain you of life; Gross, but a great metaphor. You do not have to be an expert to look at a leaf and ask your child, "How does it make energy? How do you re-energize?"

Over time examples from nature can provide a cross-over to emotional and social interactions. The child learns their impact on the patterns of social interactions. Our family headed out to the library and to get ice cream. I could feel the tension as I climbed into the car. One child was pushing everyone past their ability to settle. I brought him inside and acknowledged that everyone felt like a level 5 hurricane. I asked him what impacts a hurricane in scientific terms. At first, he said, "me," - which was funny and true in this scenario, but the response deflects blame instead of accepting responsibility. Blame yourself and everyone else for making you feel bad. So I prompted him, "In science, what impacts a hurricane?" He thought and said, "Wind, if it hits land, temperature." I affirmed those and then said, "So if a hurricane can downgrade at any moment from a level 5 because of something shifting, what could you do to bring our category 5 family hurricane down instead of escalating it?" He gave an example of ignoring someone snapping at him. I affirmed that was a good idea and suggested he give everyone a jolly rancher because sometimes a treat can also downgrade a "hurricane". I thanked him for being a weather changer. Using nature targets a different area of the brain. This alternate route avoids the traditional trigger spots that may place a child on the defense.

-Connection to Dissociative Parts

These are some activities we have used that are more direct in approaching dissociation and different self-states. These activities require curiosity and compassion and should occur when the child and adult feel regulated. Some of these activities fit a therapeutic environment, and others could be a family activity.

-Introduce yourself

Supplies needed- Folded paper in the shape of a little book and drawing utensils.

We have a large timeline that shows each person's life points within our blended family. Since our children were moved frequently in their younger years to different homes, there is a lack of pictures and memorable stories. When they ask questions, we only have a little documentation about their first 5 or so years. Part of reconstructing that history has been coming up with stories. "What type of birthday party do you think 3-year-old you had?" "What age do you think you walked?" And we come up with some common questions for each age of them. Making these little booklets is a way to introduce any internal ages to their current "oldest" age. These are basic and include favorite foods, colors, tv shows, and any known life experiences. The goal is for any inner younger ages to know they are safe and welcome, that the eldest age supports them, and that imagination is a safe conduit for information.

This activity can be modified and applied in a variety of situations. For diagnosed kids, the booklet can, "Introduce the real me!" They can highlight their interests and characteristics that may get lost behind their daily work on "issues" or diagnosis-related topics. Another application is for a child who lives deeply in imagination or creative existence - they introduce their world and important F.A.Q.'s that others need to know about them.

What makes me

Supplies needed - nesting dolls or other nesting-style toys and drawing supplies. I used animal nesting dolls instead of Russian Matrushka dolls, as I wanted them to cross-apply neutrally to any demographic of my kids. I also found a soft-sided toddler toy shaped like an igloo with multiple stuffed penguins that fit inside.

Discuss emotions and "parts of us" with your kids using these for visuals. "Do you ever feel sad and happy at the same time?" "How does the largest animal help the littlest one speak and feel safe?" Let your kids expand on any emotions they feel. If drawing this on paper, note if any feelings are illustrated bigger or smaller than others, the intensity of the coloring, etc.

"Sometimes when hard or bad things happen, we can hide a part of us to feel safe" and visually show safe-hiding with nesting dolls. Have an open-ended discussion on why this may be and what needs to happen for the other part to be able to be out on its own. Another question may be, "Do you ever feel kind, but your muscles feel like kicking something?" And talk about our emotions and bodies doing conflicting things. This aims to introduce the idea that we are multi-faceted and have many things happening inside our brains and bodies. We want to normalize being human and have varied experiences and defense mechanisms.

How my brain works

Basic brain awareness empowers your child to know they can make choices in this process and not feel like "all this is happening TO me". We refer to neural pathways as brain bridges- when the kids are stressed and unable to communicate, we can say, "Hold on, your brain bridge is backlogged; give it a chance to clear!" If your child knows that their brain dissociates to disconnect from painful or uncomfortable situations, they can learn their brain is working to protect them. Gaining vocabulary to advocate for themselves is ultimately empowering and develops self-trust. The tv show, Phineas and Ferb, had an episode where the friends traveled through Candace, their sister's brain. It took them through different zones and is a fun visual of how our brains work. See the resources list for two great books by Lori Desautels on Neuroscience and children.

Mindfulness/Awareness

Goal: Teach the child how to be aware- start with noticing externally, then can shift to internally.

Building a capacity for mindfulness should start small and then expand. Mindfulness is to be mindful of what the body and mind are experiencing. I started with having the kids sit outside for one minute at a time - we had to build from zero. I would challenge them to feel the breeze on their cheeks, listen to the birds, feel the bumpy concrete, or wet grass under their toes. Observing with our senses does not need a judgment of "I like or don't like". Once they built their capacity, we incorporated nature journals and would sit for longer periods. Some days this would feel like "just one more thing to do." Especially with kids who push back at everything, it can feel like a challenge. The benefit, though, is enormous. Helping a child to identify what they are physically experiencing in a neutral moment, like being outside for 1 minute, is the foundation for them learning to recognize the physical sensations connected to emotions and protection. A child who can't recognize feeling a breeze on their face will have difficulty identifying a prickly feeling that warns them something is wrong or butterflies that are for excitement and not fear.

Some kids and adults have learned that silence is scary - the quiet before a violent storm or a deafening silence of rejection/desertion. Quiet may feel difficult, lonely, and even dangerous. Creating safe moments for quiet and stillness is challenging for an activated body. Part of disorganized neural organization is when the brain gives a cue for calm; the amygdala may override that cue and instead alert the body to danger. Instead of following a predictable neural pathway, the body may start causing chaos to achieve calm or self-soothing. If the children seem unable to maintain a calm, use tactile objects to rub on the skin or do some stretches to draw their mind's focus to the sensory experience. I must remind myself, "It is a safety threat for a child who was forgotten or neglected to sit quietly without a caregiver's acknowledgment." Over time, mindfulness and environmental awareness will help the feeling that silence or calm does not equate to being forgotten.

Later we progress to awareness of hard feelings like disappointment and sadness. Sometimes we have to practice these emotions. Using mindful prompts can help them to experience disappointment that is not drowning. The caregiver does not give solutions or redirections but draws awareness to where the body holds a physical response to the emotional experience. "Wow! My neck tightens up when I feel angry! What about you? Where does your body feel it?" Building a capacity for good feelings can be challenging for people who have experienced so much disappointment. Choosing a calm feeling- swaying back and forth, rubbing a soft blanket on their arm, listening to someone laugh- and practicing it together builds the capacity for good feelings. For kids who have developed asynchronously, experienced trauma, and/or were shamed for feelings or body responses when younger- mindfulness can feel dangerous if not gently guided through by a trusted person. The

ANP must help regulate the inner child parts- as calming strategies can trigger their separated selves.

Shadow

When there are consistent intrusive thoughts that surface, we have used a visualization that involves a shadow. Depending on your child's needs, you could include a flashlight and act it out in the physical world or through visualization. This activity helps to determine "Are the thoughts mine or someone else's?" For example, the child had negative interactions with peers at school and has the ongoing thought, "No one likes me, and I have no friends."

We visualize ourselves standing in a dark room (a quiet, peace-filled room) and then picture a light starting to shine like the sun rising. As it rises, they look to see where the shadow is. As the light rises, the shadow should change (just like in the actual world). Once the light is straight overhead, we pause and talk about the warmth on our skin and try to connect it to a physical sensation. Then I will ask (with the light overhead) where they see the shadow now. If the shadow is still long, with the light overhead, then it is not their shadow. It is like the shadow from Peter Pan; it's an external formation. My kids already knew the science of shadows, but this may require some pre-explanation. Then we explore who or where that voice could be coming from. If the shadow is "hidden" when the light is straight above, it is from within ourselves.

Another way to tell if the shadow/voice is from an internal source is if the shadow connects to them. It is not from their center of origination if the shadow and feet are not connected. This picture gives a "reality" they can grasp on their own. "When a thought of _____ comes up, check in and see where the shadow is." Hyper-perceptive children will unintentionally absorb other people's thoughts and intents and will not learn to distinguish until they are much older. This activity empowers them to do self-checks on their own time. It follows a natural scientific "law" of existence. When there is an adaption or a morph from that, it is an indicator that there is another part that needs alignment.

Balloon forest

This strategy came up when working with a part of my child that was very detached. This part presents itself in a consistently clueless way. By clueless, I mean it had little awareness of time, common phrases, memories, or present interactions. This part of them would be unaware of how 3 days differed from 6 months. Commonplace conversations would suddenly be unknown territory for him. I realized that this part of the child was restless, unsettled, and flighty because it had zero narrative to give them roots. It had so many questions but no way to formulate them or to find answers. It had no grasp on time and could not absorb a narrative timeline of his memories or future planning. It's like this part functioned in a "zero-gravity" zone. There was nothing to ground it or rise to, just float through existence. In this self-state, they would jump from topic to topic frantically. The other kids in my house had a tough time with this state - simply because it never made sense. When told, "We already have talked about this," the child would giggle and laugh, a default response of disconnect yet self- preservation.

We did a visualization of picturing all the thoughts, memories, and experiences from his 5-year-old self-state as balloons. These were all floating around; they couldn't find a place to attach. Our first step was to attach strings to them and then tie them to the ground, they simply needed to be grounded in order to be accessed. We also reminded his other self-state (3-year-old) that this was the 5-year-old's forest of bal-loons. We agreed, with a giggle, that sometimes 3-year-olds like to pop balloons, but the 5-year-old did not want the balloons popped. This assertion of pecking order is essential for the internal parts to align in a way that honors boundaries, abilities, and age states.

After mentally tying the strings to the ground to root all his memo-ries, I asked him to identify the color of the balloons that held positive memories for the 5-year-old. In my mind's eye, I saw the color pink, but I needed him to affirm what he was experiencing. He said pink, so I knew we were on the same page. I explained that I could see (in my mind's eye) many other colored balloons- green, red, purple- all holding other memories that we were not ready to look at yet. We didn't need to fear them floating away because they were rooted and contained in their safe spaces. Remember: the brain moves toward healing and acceptance if we give it the safe, supportive space to do so.

He then asked about the "blue balloons" because they seemed calm. I intuitively knew these were positive memories from the 5-year-old's past. Though positive, we needed to root the 5-year-old's current reality before it could visit those memories. I explained to him that even though those were positive memories, we needed to follow the timeline and first give the 5-year-old stories about its 5-year-old life, then we could jump to the past. We want him to conceptualize time and understand where each thing has its place. I encouraged the 5-year-old self- state to find a pink balloon whenever they felt overwhelmed, had questions, or were uncertain. It could find a balloon on its own and discover a memory to talk about. Over the next few weeks, we supplemented this with pictures, timelines, and stories. Each self-state needs to build capacity, develop an awareness of sensations/emotions, and then develop maturity.

Safe spaces

Creating a safe mental space can be an effective strategy for helping a child set internal boundaries. An internal safe spot will help a dissociated child choose when to disconnect in overwhelming situations connectedly. This empowering process gives a child consent and support when they need to disconnect.

Drawing on paper or creating with playdough are ways to encourage children to develop this mental safe space. We internalize this strategy by mentally picturing the safe space. The child can picture any container- a treasure box, Pringles can, playhouse, etc. The child can be as creative or basic as they like. Ideas, thoughts, and memories can all be placed in this internal safe space. For myself, I picture a backpack similar to Dora the Explorer's backpack. It can safely keep my ideas, recurring thoughts, and things that feel urgent but are not. My back- pack has tools and resources to help me know how to respond and filter out what I need to address first. Sometimes I prefer journalling my internal list, but I find that intrusive thoughts and processing of memories benefit from having a safe space to "sit in."

One child had an angry part that we connected with highly disruptive and dangerous behaviors at night. Doing a mental visualization, the child described this part as a tiger- prowling and somewhat dangerous. We worked together for the child to mentally visualize and create a safe mental space for this tiger to live. The child provided it with lots of toys and food. They made sure it had buttons to ask for help. And all the other internal parts of the child had locks they could reach to ensure it was safe inside. The tiger was important when trying to protect the child, but its prowling during calm moments would leave the self-states frantic. Particularly at night when the child needed to be sleeping. By creatively developing an internal safe space, the child is nurturing themself. They recognize the need for play, nourishment, and connection and begin to develop boundaries. It is these smaller steps that help the child to learn that their entire self is valuable. We do not need to reject a disruptive part but need to help the child create a safe boundary for themself.

For some kids, this concept of an internal safe space may feel distressing. If they have a high level of shame and self-distrust, they may need to use an external "holding space" until they can safely build an internal space. This can look like writing on a piece of paper and putting it in a safe jar, wearing different color bracelets to signify switches, or using a code system.

Team Challenge

Team challenge is when the child works with their internal parts to accomplish a goal. Adults do this by re-parenting or re-playmate themselves. A child can be a team with their inner fractured parts - strategize, celebrate, and encourage.

-An example of a tangible goal is when one of my children wants to learn how to carve wood. Given the history of unpredictable, dangerous choices, I had been unwilling to buy whittling tools. After seeing their development progress, I bought some tools. As we discussed using them safely, I could sense a restlessness growing. I initially could not tell if it was my own anxiety, his excitement, or something else. Pausing, I could see in my mind's eye what felt like his 3-year-old self watching excitedly. It also felt like a different "shame part" was anticipating an injury and looking for ways to sabotage. I felt hesitant- I did not want the child to get hurt, I did not want them to make a choice that could cause further self-distrust, and I did not want to feel anxious and hyper-vigilant. I wanted the child to try a new skill and learn they can make responsible choices. Because we already used language surrounding "internal parts," we talked about the 3-year-old feeling curious but not being a safe activity for them. We brainstormed a few guidelines: the 3-year-old could ask questions but not touch, the child's eldest age was in charge, and if they felt foggy-brained, they needed to stop whittling. Not all selves will be in a frame of mind to participate or create a safe environment. We showed compassion to its jumble of feelings (excitement mixed with heavy anxiety) and then reaffirmed that the 9-year-old was in charge. Though I supervised the whittling, my son felt calm and was in charge of himself and all his parts.

Self-accountability Prompts

It is essential to give self-accountability questions to kids who experience dissociation. These questions are helpful for any kid - but a child, who experiences dissonance between external and internal prompts, needs a framework to realign themselves. As they become more independent, their ANP and inner selves will be responsible for their self-correction, self-acceptance, and self-trust. Many dissociated individuals experience gaslighting (when someone convinces them that what they are experiencing is not real). These self-accountability prompts help keep oneself in check in environments where they don't have a trustworthy person to check in with.

- *"What do I already know? What can I predict?"*

Transitions. Transitions are challenging when transitioning from media to free time, school to home, or different parents being in charge. Unpredictability can flare up anxiety within a child from a high-stress environment, neurodivergent children who need assistance with recall, and the adults with the responsibility to facilitate these transitions. As much as possible, transitions should be clear and stated in advance - regardless if it is a substitute teacher, babysitter, change of plans, or change in schedule. This advance notice reduces the adrenaline rush that may come with unpredicted changes. Giving a time estimate also helps the child's prediction and planning skills. (For example, we will have a substitute teacher for two classes. Or, this week, our dinners will be at 7:00 instead of 6:00. Next week, we will return to 6:00 dinners.)

The children had several concerns when we first started going to the library's downtown branch. They could list out some predictions (there will be books, it will take longer to get there, we might get ice cream after), and there were some worries (what if they don't have the book I need, what if I get lost, there are a lot of homeless people). They are such great problem-solvers; I love supporting their ability to address their own worries. Answering their own needs affirms to their inner parts that their Being (body, mind, soul) is equipped with incredible resources! This internal resourcing strategy is essential in healing complex PTSD and ongoing traumas and equipping and building confidence in neuro-divergent individuals. I offer solutions for situations where we may still have hesitance. Over time, their worries can become optimistic predictions. For example, we have never had a negative experience with any of the homeless individuals. Now, they are part of the prediction, not the worry. And the kids have curiosity surrounding homelessness, survival, housing, and food provision. Curiosity is a huge indicator of self-trust and expanded capacity. When fears have a pathway into curiosity, that is incredible growth.

-*Social interactions*. ADHD, ASD, PTSD, and other neuro-divergent brains can have difficulty reading and interpreting social cues. A hyper-vigilant child will be looking for danger/threat in every inter-action. A child who misses cues may disproportionately experience stressful interactions because they are not interpreting social signals or their intent. Reflecting on predictions, patterns, and general societal rules can provide a mental framework for kids that struggle to interpret social cues. School fights are an example of a discussion we have had at home. Three of my children went into 7th and 8th grade following a year of e-learning from the pandemic. As they got used to school, they were shocked by the number of altercations happening in the hallways and at lunch. Some of my children were terrified of being fought them-selves, and they all felt on edge.

We had a big family meeting where they vented frustrations with kids, teachers, and the chaos. The venting then shifted into more vul-nerable sharing about not feeling safe, not knowing how to fight back, and constantly feeling on guard. As a caregiver, I feel myself getting geared up and ready to confront the administration- however, I also recognize that stems from feeling helpless within these situations. Their dad and I started to ask them to make some predictions. These are not true across the board, but fights frequently happen with someone smaller wanting to fight someone bigger; someone will generally tell you in advance or send signals beforehand. As we made some predictions, the kids started to feel more relaxed and could get curious, recognizing some of their own predictions. "Wait, if I am just staring at them, they might think I'm challenging them to a fight?" "Oh, if it's happening across the cafeteria, then it probably won't come over by me?" "Most of the fights seem to be about boyfriends and girlfriends, and I am not dating anyone, so I can't steal anyone!" We also discussed practical strategies like contacting their school counselor, ways to disrupt a fight, and positioning themselves safely.

-*Self-accountability*: My kids with ADHD often lose sight of where they are supposed to be and what they are supposed to be doing. Layer that with dissociative inner parts - life can get chaotic. I want them to develop intrinsic checks as they grow older instead of having to check in externally. If they answer "no" to these questions, then they self-correct. Sometimes I will prompt you to count to 5, then check your brain! Our brains even store information yet to be processed. Frequently they can pause, access their peripheral brain and find the answer.

1. Am I where I'm supposed to be?
2. Am I doing what I'm supposed to be doing?
3. Do I have the materials I'm supposed to have?
4. Do I know the instructions?

-*Self-check with the environment*: We make predictions about the environment we will be in. As they age, they need the skill set to make these predictions and self-check questions independently. Every environment has different rules and expectations. You can discuss these with your kids and adapt the questions as you see fit! I will use the library as an example:

1. What type of setting? Informal or formal, observational or participatory, flexible or rigid. The library is informal but has rules; you participate by getting books, and you should not run.

2. What is the energy? If it is a sacred quiet library or a library that encourages loud laughter- you can match the energy of the environment.

3. What are 75% of the people doing? There will always be outliers within group environments. If you are not aligned with 75% of the people- you need to evaluate if you are not fitting the setting correctly. There is a time and place for not fitting in. Most people will gather books or work on computers at the library, and some will sleep or eat.

4. What are the societal or cultural norms? Respect for an environment also requires awareness of cultural norms. Some individuals carry bags of their belongings at the library due to housing insecurity. We talk about not staring at the bags or laughing at clothes because this is a norm. It is also another norm in the city to ignore loud hollers, unless directed at you. If someone is talking to themself or yelling, you can ignore them, send peace vibes and go on with your book finding.

Returning the Stories

Kids who were forced to take on their parents' role will have stories in them that do not belong to them. Whether from an epigenetic, ancestral, or intergenerational perspective - stories live in our bodies of those who came before. Kids who have multiple parts will sometimes have emotional or bodily memories of experiences that did not happen to them. "Returning the Stories" is a way to reclaim the child's autonomy and return a story line to its original owner. The parent or grandparent can not fully heal if their stories have been spread to the winds. A sibling that shares trauma bonds may hold on to another sibling's story as a form of protection.

This "returning" could be done through visualization, drawing or writing. You could even dance or sing - do what feels right to you. For me, I visualized the stories as books on an internal bookshelf. I visualized the person they belonged to and gathered up these stories. In my mind's eye I told them about the treasures in their stories and how they were the caretaker of their own stories. I set a boundary of not being caretaker of their books anymore. Mentally, I encouraged them to gather up their own stories so they would have all the pieces of their puzzle. Over time, you can become practiced in recognizing which stories belong on your shelf, which influence your life, and which belong to someone else.

Dissociation Focused:
Looking Through the Eyes of Trauma and Dissociation, Sandra Paulsen Ph. D.
When There Are No Words, Sandra Paulsen Ph. D.
Healing the Fractured Child, Frances S. Waters DCSW, LMSW, LMFT

Children's Books about Dissociative Disorders:
Rob the Robin and the Bald Eagle, Madge Bray
The Patchwork Quilt, J.D. Clark

Parenting/Caregiver, Teacher Resources:
Beyond Consequences Logic and Control 1, 2. Heather T. Forbes LCSW
Connections Over Compliance, Lori L. Desautels, Ph. D
Intentional Neuroplasticity, Lori L. Desautels, Ph.D.

Adult Focused:
Adult Children of Emotionally Immature Parents, Lindsay C. Gibson, PsyD
Burnout: The Secret to Unlocking Stress Cycle, Emily Nagoski, PhD Amelia Nagoski,   DMA
Call of the Wild, Kimberly Ann Johnson
Healing Developmental Trauma, Laurence Heller, PhD Aline LaPierre, PsyD
My Grandmother's Hands, Resma Menaakem

"Neuron Number and Size in Prefrontal Cortex of Children with Autism", 2011.

https://pubmed.ncbi.nlm.nih.gov/22068992/. Eric Courchesne 1, Peter R Mouton, Michael E Calhoun, Katerina Semendeferi, Clelia Ahrens-Barbeau, Melo- die J Hallet, Cynthia Carter Barnes, Karen Pierce

Rachel Heinbaugh is a juggler of multiple roles. A mom to 5 kids, vintage clothes seller, chaotic gardener, wife, author, and reluctant laundry folder. Her house is maximalist and fully lived in. She is an ordained Unitarian Minister with training in inner healing. Holding a Bachelor's degree in Biblical Studies, Sign Language Interpreting, a M. Ed. in Instructional Design, and is a N.A.R.M. Informed Professional (Neuro Affective Relational Model). Rachel enjoys observing systems to find gaps and build bridges between the theoretical and practical. Rachel seeks to create safe spaces for families to process their relationships in a healthy way. You can contact Rachel at www.indyroots.com.